HISTORY, THE ANATOMY
OF TIME

The Final Phase of Sunlight

BOŽIDAR KNEŽEVIĆ
(1862-1905)

BOZIDAR KNEŽEVIĆ

HISTORY, THE ANATOMY OF TIME

The Final Phase of Sunlight

Translated by
Dr. George Vid Tomashevich
Professor of Anthropology
Buffalo State University College

in collaboration
with
Dr. Sherwood A. Wakeman

And with a preface by
Dr. W. Warren Wagar
Professor of History
State University of New York
at
Binghamton

Philosophical Library
New York

This text is a translation from the original Serbo-Croatian *Principi istorije (Principles of History)*. The present title given to the work is taken from Knežević's aphorisms (numbered herein 7 and 12).

Library of Congress Catalog Card No. 79-89888
SBN 8022-2357-5

Manufactured in the United States of America

This Translation is
Gratefully Dedicated
To the Memory
of
Helen Wakeman

Contents

TRANSLATOR'S FOREWORD

This book contains my translation from Serbo-Croatian into English of the shorter version of Božidar Knežević's *Principles of History*, a joint title of *Succession in History (Red u istoriji)*, which appeared in Belgrade in 1898, and *Proportion in History (Proporcija u istoriji)*, which came out in 1901. The two volumes together amounted to approximately 690 pages of elegant philosophical abstractions, discouragingly long and difficult for most of the likely readers. My translation is based on Kenžević's own abridgment of that considerably more voluminous original *opus*. It must be stressed, however, that the abridgment represents a carefully extracted quintessence of all the important propositions, arguments, examples and conclusions of its larger model. This authoritative condensation of the philosopher's most significant work was first published in installments in the prestigious *Serbian Literary Herald (Srpski književni glasnik)* in 1904 and then as *Two Laws in History (Dva zakona u istoriji)*, a reprint from the above journal, later the same year. In 1920, Geca Kon published a new edition of this material, entitled *The Law of Succession in History (Zakon reda u istoriji)* with an interesting and informative preface by Prof. Vladimir Vujić. In 1972, two venerable Serbian publishing houses, the *Matica srpska* and the *Srpska književna zadruga* (SKZ), prepared a single volume edition of representative selections from Knežević's philosophical works under the title of *Man and History (Čovek i istorija)* with a valuable preface by Professor Dragan Jeremić. Their volume embraces both of the author's abridgments as well as 491 of his aphorisms. The most complete collection of Knežević's *Thoughts (Misli)*, however, was prepared in 1931 by Dr. Paulina Lebl-Albala, with a still unsurpassed introductory study by Dr. Ksenija Atanasijević, distinguished Dean and *Grande Dame* of Serbian philosophy.

The present volume includes, alas, only 50 out of 876 aphorisms published in the Albala-Atanasijević edition.

I alone bear the full and exclusive responsibilty for the accuracy and faithfulness of the translation itself. As for purely literary qualities, which parts of this work undoubtedly possess, most of the credit for them belongs, of course, to Knežević himself and to my talented friend and collaborator, Dr. Sherwood A. Wakeman. His unselfish gift of time, energy, skill and knowledge, his erudite, rigorous and often creative criticism, and his tactful but firm editorial scrutiny have been invaluable from the beginning to the end of this delicate but rewarding venture.

It gives me great pleasure to acknowledge my indebtedness to Mrs. Diana Fabiano, Mr. R. Joseph Myers, and Ms. Margo Skinner for their conscientious and intelligent help in typing and retyping various phases of the evolving manuscript. Likewise, I owe sincere thanks to Mrs. Carol Janiszewski for her ungrudging, kind and efficient secretarial cooperation at a moment's notice, and to Miss Miriam Ravnik for her sensitivity and attention to detail in proofreading.

I also wish to express my deepest appreciation to my learned friends and colleagues, Dr. Antoinette

Mann Paterson, Dr. Gerhard Falk, Dr. William Engelbrecht, Dr. Simeon W. Chilungu and Dr. Lynn Rose for their incisive and encouraging critical comments after reading or listening to all, or substantial stretches, of this emerging book from a variety of scholarly viewpoints.

A special, warm gratitude is reserved for Dr. Warren Wagar whose brief but authoritative preface places Knežević in proper intellectual context and correct historical perspective and does great honor to this entire enterprise.

Finally, I want to reiterate my profound sense of obligation to members of my family, Mrs. Mara Tomasevic, Mrs. Desa Wakeman and Mr. Nicholas Tomasevic for their unflagging intellectual and moral support and generous material assistance particularly in connection with several trips to Yugoslavia, required for the completion and publication of this labor of love.

The appearance of this work in 1980 is the translator's tribute to the living spirit of a great and noble thinker on the 75th anniversary of his premature death.

G.V.T.

PREFACE

by W. Warren Wagar
State University of New York
at Binghamton

Every utterance of man, great or small, draws its substance from the thought-world of its own unique time and space. In a certain year, in a certain cultural milieu, only certain thoughts are, quite literally, thinkable. Whatever the individual mind contributes, it contributes within the finite possibilities of its age.

In the case of the Serbian philosopher Božidar Knežević, the two most powerful forces in his thought-world were German historism and Anglo-French positivism. Few social thinkers of his generation could have avoided the influence of either.

But in the late nineteenth century a small nation on the periphery of Western civilization would feel most acutely the force of positivism. Already, in the heartlands, other movements of ideas were at work, preparing the future. In Serbia positivism was still *le dernier cri,* "the latest thing."

The word itself goes back no further than the philosophy of the French polymath Auguste Comte, who died in 1857. As a world-view, positivism asserts that whatever men can know, they know through the evidence of their senses, ordered and verified by the methods of the natural and social sciences. "Sociology" is another term coined by Comte. For him it was the highest science, providing a scientific explanation of the most complex phenomenon in the universe: the behavior of *Homo sapiens* as a social animal.

In Knežević's student years, positivist ideas were invading Serbia in every department of thought. A similar process was at work, let it be noted, in another national culture still on the outskirts of Western civilization, the culture of the United States. In the same period that young scholars such as Lester Ward, John ,Fiske, and James Harvey Robinson were producing systems of positivist thought in America, Knežević was busily absorbing and propagating the positivist gospel in Serbia.

The final decades of the nineteenth century were an exhilarating time for Serbian social thought. A *mélange* of self-proclaimed positive sciences of society entered the Serbian thought-world almost simultaneously, from Marxist political economy to the equally all-encompassing philosophies of Comte and his British rival and successor Herbert Spencer. Knežević himself supplied an invaluable translation of the British positivist historian Henry Thomas Buckle's *History of Civilization in England.* Anthropologists, and many sociologists as well, were closely following and adapting the work of Charles Darwin, firmly anchored in the positivist tradition. The writings of younger Western positivists—Walter Bagehot, Paul von Lilienfeld, Albert Schäffle, Jacques Novicow, and others—were coming to be known. Everyone aspired to make the study of man a true science.

It is against this background that Knežević's exhaustive and elaborate laws of succession and proportion in history must be understood. In essence they are a striking transmutation of the synthetic philosophy of Spencer, introduced to Serbian readers in the 1880's. Spencer, too, was a great law-giver. Taking his cues from physics and Darwinian biology, Spencer constructed a vast system of social thought that traced the evolution of being from simplicity to complexity, from homogeneity to heterogeneity, from inchoate stirrings to organized and reconciled harmony, culminating in the future dissolution and collapse of a perfectly equilibrated social organism. Throughout Knežević's code of historical laws, the potent influence of Spencer is plain to see.

The keynote of both is evolutionary determinism. From simple, homogeneous, material foundations, civilization painfully evolves toward a complex harmony in which freedom, at last, is possible. But even the freedom won with such difficulties is no more than the freedom to "obey reason," to choose what the frail voice of reason prescribes; and in both systems, the point of perfect equilibrium lasts only briefly, to be succeeded by decay and degeneration, back to the primordial chaos. History follows laws ordained by the nature of things. As Knežević writes, "To reduce all the laws in all fields of human thought to [the exactness of] the laws of astronomy would be to reach the ideal stage of reason."

The doctrine of evolution shared by virtually all positivist social thinkers in the second half of the nineteenth century was blended in the thought of Knežević with *Historismus,* the historism of German idealist philosophy and German academic historiography. As evolutionary theory required all things to be measured by their place in the sequences of geological time, so historism proclaimed the relativity of all institutions and ideas to their historical context. No product of human culture made sense except in terms of its origins and development, and the actions of every man and woman were historically determined.

Positivist evolutionism, with its roots in biological thought, and historism, with its roots in the idealist philosophies of Herder and Hegel, may have contradicted one another at the level of metaphysics, but in Knežević (as perhaps in Marx) they are mutually reinforcing. Over and over, the Serbian philosopher insists on the preordained historicity of man's life. "Everything," he contends, "is just and righteous in its place and time." Everything is valuable, or in the phrase of Leopold von Ranke, "immediate to God," because it occurs at precisely the time appointed for it in the grand historical scheme of human development.

Yet the relativity in history is transcended by the wholeness of history. Like his contemporaries James Harvey Robinson in America and Henri Berr in France, Knežević enjoins the historian to take the totality of human experience for his province, leaving out nothing. For history properly conceived is a synthesis of all knowledge, a universal science that shows how all the doings of man are inextricably intertwined and justified by their common destiny. This or that individual act or idea may seem unrighteous to the ahistorical mind, but in a vision of the whole, which only world history gives, all things human find their apology.

One might just as well say: all things divine. In the final reckoning, Knežević's philosophy of history is a Hegelian theodicy, a justification of the ways of God conceived as the indwelling Logos of evolution and history. From God, the ground of being, all the well-ordered events in the dramas of nature and man proceed inexorably. It is a God that only an idealist philosopher could love, and a God in which even a materialist philosopher could believe. Certainly it is not the God of orthodox Jewish or Christian faith. But many a thinker of Knežević's generation in both Europe and America reached similar conclusions about the deity. The numerous "evolutionary" theologies of the late nineteenth century, some directly inspired by the writings of Spencer, bear ample witness.

Yet however much one might be tempted to dismiss the philosophy of Božidar Knežević as a quaint Balkan period piece, it is more than that. Its special rhetoric belongs to a dead past, but positivism and historism both survive in various modalities in the late twentieth century. The Serbian philosopher may have more to say to us than he had for the generation that immediately followed him. His vision of the integration of the world into a single sociocultural system is persuasive today, as it could not have been in the age of Hitler and Stalin. The worldwide renascence of Marxist humanism also lends fresh authority to Knežević's program for a comprehensive science of social progress grounded in historical understanding. "Human economy," he writes, "is the foundation of all society, and all later, higher social forms depend upon the nature and level of economic life." The coming transformation of the modern world-economy into a social-democratic world republic—when and if it occurs—will confirm that Božidar Knežević saw the future with far more acuity than his hopelessly reactionary forerunner, Herbert Spencer.

English-speaking readers owe much to Professor Tomashevich for his elegant translation of this remarkable work.

Božidar Knežević:
a Yugoslav Philosopher
of History

by
George Vid Tomashevich

Božidar Knežević:
a Yugoslav Philosopher
of History

'Car enfin qu'est-ce que l'homme dans la nature? Un
néant à l'égard de l'infini, un tout à l'égard du néant,
un milieu entre rien et tout. Infiniment éloigné de
comprendre les extrêmes, la fin des choses et leur
principe sont pour lui invinciblement cachés dans un
secret impénétrable, également incapable de voir le
néant d'où il est tiré, et l'infini où il est englouti.'

BLAISE PASCAL, *Pensée 72*

I

Knežević was born on March 7, 1862 in the small
town of Ub, in north-western Serbia. He was the first
child of a mild, soft-hearted shopkeeper, who died
when his son was a year old, and of a woman of nota-
ble intelligence, who remarried soon afterwards
under pressure of difficult conditions. Her second
husband was a harsh man. Of this marriage she had
five children who claimed most of her time and affection. This is why she was not able to show sufficient
tenderness towards her eldest son and to protect him
from his stepfather's cruelty. During the winter, after
returning from school, the boy had to look after his
stepfather's shop, while the man drank at a nearby

1

tavern. Many times, after hours of standing in the icy shop, Knežević was found in a frozen condition. It is understandable that such a childhood left in his memory many deep and painful scars. This is probably why he emphasizes, on more than one occasion, the overwhelming significance of childhood experiences for a man's later development and the crucial importance of earlier historical periods for the understanding of later ones.

As a student in Belgrade, where he attended gymnasium and university, Knežević earned his living as a house-servant and private tutor. Throughout his studies, despite extreme material difficulties, he was a hard-working, serious scholar. In addition to the many subjects of his heavy curriculum, he managed, by self-tuition, to master the English language.

Sleeping on snow-covered ground during the Serbo-Bulgarian war of 1885, he contracted a pulmonary catarrh which was to plague his health until the end of his days. Between 1884 and 1902 he worked as teacher and director of a gymnasium in several towns in the interior of the country. Less than three years before his death he was assigned to a teaching position in Belgrade. Thus eighteen years of his short career were spent in the isolated and drowsy small towns of 19th-century Serbia, away from the capital and its bookshops and libraries. Knežević died on March 3, 1905, when tuberculosis overcame his never robust physical constitution.

According to his widow, his former pupils and acquaintances, and an unfinished portrait in oils, he was tall and lean; his walk was upright and dignified, his expression serious; he had regular features, a long face, and an enormous forehead; his curly hair was light brown, his eyes were blue, and his moustache

and beard somewhat reddish. To some of his countrymen "he looked like an Englishman."[1]

Those who knew him remember his impeccable
behavior, his poise and elegant manners, and his
politeness, particularly towards women, about whom
he left a number of interesting aphorisms.[2]

An unhappy child, always extremely sensitive and
very reserved, burdened throughout his life with
serious financial hardships, and unable to establish a
satisfactory emotional, intellectual, and moral contact
with his fellow-countrymen, he was too unpractical,
proud, and reluctant to try to elbow his way towards a
more suitable position in the social hierarchy. In try-
ing to explain his situation to himself and to reconcile
it with his self-respect, he offers the following
rationalization: "Many more people live in the darkness of anonymity than in the daylight of publicity.
But very few are those who intentionally withdraw
into obscurity in order to see better what those in the
daylight are doing."[3] In a similar mood he observes
that the more one thinks the less one participates in
worldly affairs, and that, to accomplish something
worth while, one has to "withdraw from circulation."

But for Knežević "to withdraw from circulation"
did not mean to abandon all interest in public affairs.
Several of his aphorisms indicate that he had definite
and strong political opinions, some of which contain
an important message for the modern world. In
seeming reference to the tragic scandals of the last
Obrenovićes he observes: "The more the crown glit-

---

[1] This biographical outline is based on *Božidar Knežević*, a detailed study
in Serbo-Croatian by Ksenija Atanasijević. See *Misli*, Belgrade, 1931. See
also Vladimir Vujić's preface to B. Knežević, *Zakon reda u istoriji*, Belgrade,
1920.

[2] B. Knežević, *Misli*, p. xxxiii.

[3] *Ibid.*, aphorism 472.

ters, the more the people remain in darkness. In order for the people to be illuminated, it is sufficient for the crown to be clean."[4] In another thought he compares a bad king to a barren cloud which "makes the air stuffy but gives no rain."[5]

Deeply impressed by the British, Knežević believed that, for the time being, the best form of government was a combination of monarchy, aristocracy, and democracy. The following thought, which in the middle of this century has no less significance than it had at the time it was written, clearly emphasizes the importance of freedom for both individuals and nations: "Only in liberty does one learn to love and respect liberty as a vital necessity: only in freedom can one learn to use freedom, just as one can breathe only in the air. It is only free men and nations that know how to respect the liberty of others. As long as there are captive peoples, the free will be in danger."[6]

Although by no means a misanthrope, he was not a sociable individual. For the so-called common people, with whose hardships he sympathized, he had little personal affection. To him they were "the small change which circulates most and satisfies the most common needs of everyday living." He realized that man's spiritual culture would be impossible without the toil of these "atoms of civilization," but he was much more concerned with the fascinating problem of genius. To him, a genius was "a bill which represents the value of thousands of pieces of small change, but which seldom circulates in the market of life."[7]

His main *opus,* the *Principles of History,* so far the only attempt at a systematic philosophy of history

[4] *Ibid.,* aphorism 630.
[5] *Ibid.,* aphorism 631.
[6] *Misli,* aphorism 614.
[7] *Ibid.,* aphorism 470.

among the Southern Slavs, consists of two volumes of almost equal size. The first of them, *Succession in History* (Red u istoriji), was published in 1898; the second, *Proportion in History* (Proporcija u istoriji), in 1901. These works contain numerous philosophical postulates about the universe in which man's history takes place as well as about the laws which, according to Knežević, govern man's development. These are explained and illustrated in the course of his prolific and all-embracing argumentation which, being at times highly abstract, remains somewhat beyond the reach of the general reader. His *Thoughts* (Misli), which appeared in 1902, are much more popular and widely read and quoted among his countrymen. Rare are those educated Yugoslavs who are not familiar with at least one of this book's five successful editions. Besides many ideas borrowed from the main work, the *Thoughts* express a considerable number of condensed autobiographical insights. They embrace most of their author's opinions about the fundamental issues of religion, cosmology, ethics, and politics, and represent a precious document for the hermeneutic interpretation of Knežević's personality. For, as Wilhelm Dilthey very aptly puts it: "We can be deceived concerning the motives of action of historical personalities; even persons acting before our eyes can mislead us concerning their own motives. But the work of a great writer, a great inventor, a religious genius, or a true philosopher can never be anything other than the authentic expression of his inner life."[8]

It goes without saying that this "inner life" in turn reflects the overall economic, socio-political and intellectual conditions of an author's national background as well as his general position in the stream of history.

[8] *Le Monde de l'esprit,* Paris, 1947, p. 332.

In addition to a number of shorter essays, Knežević is the author of a lengthy study entitled *The Process of the History of Mankind and its Relation to the Other Sciences* and of an *Historical Calendar* which served as a textbook. His work in the field of translation represents a huge amount of labor: besides Buckle's voluminous *History of Civilisation in England,* Carlyle's *Lectures on Heroes and Hero-worship,* and Macaulay's *Essays on Milton and Bacon,* Knežević translated also from French, German, and Russian.[9]

Like Njegoš, he was keenly conscious of the difficulties that a genius has to overcome when born in a small country. Besides, he could hardly help being aware of the extraordinary importance of his creative activities, particularly in a *milieu* in which he had to pioneer in more than one field of speculative thought and expression. Although systematically obstructed by persons who should have welcomed his efforts and placed him in a more fitting social position, Knežević devoted his entire life to his thoughts and spent a considerable portion of a meagre income on his purely abstract pursuits.

When one thinks of the shortness of his life and the hardships under which he worked, one can hardly fail to experience a feeling of admiration for the mental and moral effort that went into his thoughts, and for his courageous and consistent striving not to allow a

---

[9] Ksenija Antanasijević, *Božidar Knežević,* in *Misli* p. viii. See also Ksenija Atanasijević, *Bibliografija radova Božidara Kneževića, Zivot i rad,* XII, 1932. See also Bibliography at the end of this volume.

With slight modifications this introductory essay originally appeared in *The Slavonic and East European Review* of the University of London, Vol. XXXV, No. 85, June 1957. The author gratefully acknowledges reprint permission.

tragically uncomfortable and always disturbed national environment to upset his calm attitude to the universe and his pananthropic, cosmopolitan point of view in relation to the history of man.

Unlike Spengler and Toynbee, Knežević was not concerned with the "decline of the West" or with its salvation from the internal and external proletariats by a penitent return to the Savior. He did not see the history of mankind either as a succession of discrete, self-contained, and impenetrable organisms or a series of twenty-one isolated units of study and sociological comparison. In Knežević's philosophy of history one can find no trace either of Spengler's ethnocentrism or of Toynbee's parochialism. Rather, his attitude is reminiscent of that taken by Kant in his *Idea for a Universal History from the Cosmopolitan Point of View*.[10]

Although not overlooking the autonomy of the world of man which, with its growing emancipation from the wider world of nature, represents the proper subject-matter of history in the narrower sense of the word, Knežević was primarily interested in history as the history of everything. He compares developments in the universe with those of the earth and the phenomena of the inorganic and organic worlds with those of mental life. But such a cosmic view does not reward him with "the cold comfort of a mechanical formula."[11] The moral issues of existence were always paramount in his mind, and no measure of his own deterministic and relativistic speculation could lull in him a disturbing awareness of the perplexity of the ontological problem of good and evil.

[10] *Idee zu einer allgemeinen Geschichte in weltbürgerlicher Absicht*, 1784.
[11] Carl Becker, *Everyman his own Historian*, pp. 179–85.

And, while he would not agree that the hundreds of thousands of years which preceded the last six thousand are less worthy of our attention than these, he would undoubtedly agree that the past few millennia of man's recorded history are certainly more interesting to us, because they display man's growing consciousness and freedom and can be "measured by the standards of human desires, purposes, and aspirations."[12]

According to Knežević, "History is an organized complex of all human sentiments, thoughts, souls, spirits, and times. In order to understand the life of man from the perspective of history, one must comprehend all the forces which influenced mankind in all times. . . . All peoples and states, all religions, literatures and philosophies, all sciences and epochs, are only the individual parts, organs, forces, and episodes of that one great whole—Universal History."[13]

In such a history of mankind Knežević discerns an ascent and a descent. He sees a development from the continuity of unconscious chaos, through the struggle and discontinuity of historical evolution, to the pinnacle of consciousness, freedom, and morality, and from there, through a reverse process of disintegration and involution, back to the continuity of unconscious chaos. His scheme of history is neither a straight line, like that of Christian theology, nor a complete circle of eternal recurrence, like that of Nietzsche and the pre-Socratics. It is rather a single semicircle, whose ascending half represents the evolution from disproportion to proportion, from ignorance to knowledge, from injustice to justice, and from

[12] *Ibid.*
[13] B. Knežević, *Zakon proporcije u istoriji,* chapter XIII, pp. 141–2. The English version is a quotation from a translation by George V. Tomashevich and Sherwood A. Wakeman, published in this volume.

blind necessity to self-conscious freedom. The descending half represents the return from the pinnacle of consciousness and understanding to the abyss of ultimate chaos.

This semicircular scheme of history, with only one beginning and only one end, results from Knežević's belief that, in accordance with the law of identity, whatever happens has to happen at a particular point in time and space; that no two phenomena can coincide with each other both spatially and temporally, and that those phenomena which coincide with each other in time alone or in space alone can be regarded at the most only as resembling each other, but never as being fully identical. From this point of view every event is of necessity unique and, while there may be eternal recurrence in terms of similarity, there can be none in terms of identity.

In its assumption of progress and its replacement of the religious faith in salvation and judgment by the belief in ever greater improvements whereby history is supposed to justify and redeem itself, Knežević's philosophy of history is doubtless one of those which, in the words of Karl Löwith, "secularize an originally theological pattern."[14] But this "secularization" remains only partial in Knežević. Like other modern interpretations of history, his is unconsciously and indirectly also of Christian origin, but it is neither anti-Christian nor pro-Christian in consequence; for, as we shall see later, although Knežević's "secularized eschatology" retains the Christian implication of a beginning and an end, he does not regard Christianity or any other religion as the sole repository of the whole truth.

[14] K. Löwith, *Meaning in History*, 1949. "Introduction," pp. 17–19, and "Progress vs. Providence: Comte," pp. 67–91.

In a very broad and all-embracing manner, this may be regarded as the skeleton of Knežević's explanation of universal history. Before examining his philosophy in greater detail, let us briefly consider its purpose.

II

Unlike Droysen's *Historik*, whose task was to establish the laws of historical investigation and knowledge rather than those of objective history,[15] Knežević's work is neither a study of the method of historical scholarship nor a formulation of a philosophy of history in the ordinary sense of the word. In so far as he deals with them at all, methodological considerations and opinions are only implicit in his propositions. Explicit throughout them is solely his intention of reaching with the aid of reason alone the limits of knowledge accessible to man, and to determine, if possible, amidst the primeval and permanent flux of the universe, the position and rank of man and the ultimate meaning of his destiny.[16]

For Knežević, as for Vico, Hegel, and Croce, philosophy and history are synonymous.[17] "As it becomes more and more the only philosophy of the human mind, history continually draws all things into itself, occupying the fields of all the other sciences, and making everything human and earthly historical."[18] His primary interest is not in personalities; he does not deal with "races, tribes, peoples, and states,

---

[15] J. Wach (*Das Verstehen*, Tübingen, 1933, p. 156): "Nicht die Gesetze der Geschichte, aber die Gesetze des historischen Erkennens und Wissens hat Droysen nach seinen Worten festhalten wollen."

[16] Ks. Atanasijević, preface to B. Knežević, *Misli*, p. xi.

[17] B. Croce, *History as the Story of Liberty*, London, 1949, pp. 14, 147–50.

[18] B. Knežević, *Zakon reda u istoriji*, XXIV, p. 83.

but only with man at various levels of historical existence, in various regions and times."[19] This conception of history as the career of one man is present
already in Pascal who urges that ". . . the whole se-
quence of men in the course of so many centuries
should be regarded as one and the same man who
always subsists and learns continually."[20] We en-
counter a similar idea in Burckhardt's *Reflections on
History,* where he observes that the spirit of man "presents itself to us as the life of one human being."[21]

While in Burckhardt history is little more than
mere continuity, whose reasonableness is beyond our
reach, in Knežević all historical events and processes
make sense only in so far as they converge on an
ultimate end. He would agree with Droysen that "the
secret of all movement or motion is its end . . ." and
that "without the consciousness of ends and of the
highest end, without the Theodicy of History, its continuity would be a mere motion in a circle repeating
itself."[22] Knežević's analogy between the individual
human being and mankind as a whole includes "the
highest end," the realization of freedom, justice, and
humaneness, in a mature, united humanity, as the
goal towards which it is worth striving, in spite of the
prospect that, like all things born, mankind too will
have to die, just as individual human beings continue
to strive for certain ends and ideals in spite of the
certainty of ultimate death.

To be able to present so broadly conceived a picture
of the history of mankind, Knežević found it necessary to consider first the entire history of nature. As

[19] *Ibid.*
[20] B. Pascal, *Pensées et opuscules* (ed. Brunschvigg), p. 80.
[21] J. Burckhardt, *Reflections on History,* London, 1950, p. 218.
[22] J. G. Droysen, *Principles of History* (Grundriss der Historik), Boston, 1893, pp. 33, 34.

other naturalistic historians, he never denied that "historical facts do not belong to the same type as physical facts."[23] He was aware of the truth that historical documents and monuments are not mere physical things, that they have to be read as symbols; but he also knew that "the human world is not a separate entity or a self-dependent reality."[24] "As the history of mankind is the last and most complicated result of all the vital forces of nature, in order to understand the history of man, one must know the entire history of nature."[25]

Nevertheless Knežević emphasizes on several occasions that in course of time "man creates more and more a separate, inner world of freedom, the realm of the humane (oblast humanoga), by constantly clearing a particular road for himself through the life of things in general."[26] The content of his concept of "the realm of the humane" is strongly reminiscent of Dilthey's idea of "the world of the spirit" (die geistige Welt) as well as of Droysen's conception of "the moral world" as the proper sphere and subject of historical investigation.

As he attempts to base his thinking about evolution and progress in the history of the universe, including "the realm of the humane," on a stable metaphysical foundation. Knežević encounters the difficulty which, in the words of Ksenija Atanasijević, accompanies every intellectual effort to "plunge into the essence of reality"—the impossibility of adequately expressing the relations of things by means of words.[27] In an

[23] E. Cassirer, *An Essay on Man*, New York, 1953, p. 255.
[24] *Ibid.*
[25] B. Knežević, *Zakon proporcije u istoriji*, Belgrade, 1920, XIII, p. 141.
[26] Vladimir Vujić, preface to B. Knežević, *Zakon reda u istoriji*, pp. xv–xvi.
[27] K. S. Atanasijević, Preface to B. Knežević, *Misli*, p. xii.

attitude characteristic of Kant and later, with modifications, also of Spencer, he admits that things not yet
investigated or beyond investigation must remain a
matter of faith. The enigma of the universe filled him
with awe, as it did Pascal. An insatiable thirst however
to examine at least what is accessible to philosophy
always drove him on. "The world," he says, "is a system of things, philosophy a system of thoughts; in
relation to the world of reality philosophy stands as a
map of the earth in relation to the earth itself; the
more profound the philosophy, the more precise is
the map."[28]

III

One of Knežević's fundamental doctrines is his
theory of truth. He claims that the difference between
error and truth is not a difference in kind, but only in
degree. "Truth is the determination of the precise
limits of things in space and time; the more precise
the limits, the higher the truth."[29] Thus, heliocentric-
ity is a higher truth than geocentricity. Similarly, the
theory of evolution is a higher truth than the doctrine
of direct and separate acts of creation. "It follows that
error is nothing but a lack of precise knowledge as to
the limits of things. Error is to truth what the child is
to the adult man, the savage to the civilized . . . the
tribe to the nation, the nation to mankind. The idea
of man can be true only in the whole of mankind;
only in mankind can one be a man."[30]

But, as everything is true only within the limits of its

[28] *Ibid.*, aphorism 105.
[29] B. Knežević, *Zakon reda u istoriji*, p. 63.
[30] *Ibid.*, pp. 61–2.

time and place, things which once were regarded as truths may, in the judgment of posterity, appear as errors. "The entire truth does not rest in any particular theory, idea or principle, as these are only particles of the whole truth."[31] And as the highest truth is one, changeless, and eternal, whatever is transient is not a complete truth.[32] Accordingly, "the highest truth cannot be found in any one man, or one people, one religion, philosophy or science, or concerned with individual times, or particular places."[33] Whatever therefore is a part of empirical reality, which is of necessity passing and ephemeral, can be only relatively true.

From the empirical point of view however Knežević maintains that every historically conditioned opinion (and every opinion is necessarily so conditioned), the later and riper it is, reconciles within itself an ever greater number of errors. Hence, at the peak of its maturity, "one mankind will reconcile within itself all the successive errors of its earlier epochs."[34] And "as the highest truth that the human mind can attain is only in the whole history of man," it follows that "only the understanding of all history can reconcile all those contrasts which successively appeared in time—the controversies between thoughts and things, man and nature, spirit and matter, freedom and destiny."[35] Although Kenžević probably died unaware of the work of Wilhelm Dilthey, some of his basic views are in striking agreement with those of the German thinker. "The finiteness of every historical phenomenon," says Dilthey, "be it a religion, an ideal or a philosophical

[31] *Ibid.*
[32] *Ibid.*
[33] *Ibid.*, p. 63.
[34] *Ibid.*, p. 68.
[35] *Ibid.*

system, and, consequently, the relativity of every human interpretation of the relation of things, is the last word of the historical conception of this world, where all is in a state of flux, where nothing is stable."[36]

Like Dilthey, Knežević also experienced the tragic conflict between dogmatism, which he could not accept in any disguise, and relativism, which fails to provide a universally valid criterion of historical judgment and understanding. Undoubtedly, he would have sympathized with Dilthey's predicament, when the old man, on his seventieth birthday, had to record the following: "The historical conception of the world liberates the human mind from the last chain which natural sciences and philosophy have not yet broken. But where are we to find the means of overcoming the anarchy of opinions which threaten to spread?"[37]

But, while Dilthey hoped that what he was unable to overcome might be overcome by his disciples, Knežević tried to convince himself that "the struggle for the ideals of mankind" might somehow supply a reliable and universally acceptable set of standards for historical evaluation and criticism. He overlooked, of course, that, no matter how reasonable and noble his own ideals and values might appear to him, they were not necessarily in agreement with those of the rest of humanity.

He was aware of the fact that every attempt on his part to understand the experiences of man implied inevitable judgment, but he continued to maintain the very delicate position that to disapprove of something is not necessarily to condemn it. "The historical understanding increasingly contracts the spheres of

---

[36] *Le Monde de l'esprit,* I (Trans. M. Remy), Paris, 1947, p. 15.
[37] W. Dilthey, *Le Monde de l'esprit,* I, p. 15.

condemnation, ridicule, stupidity, and grief, and constantly expands those of justice and right."[38] He also asserts that "by realizing that all things are necessary in the limits of their place and time, that all of them have value within those limits, one renders justice to all of them."[39]

In Knežević's *Thoughts* there is a clear indication that, though he did not like to moralize and preach, he could not fully accept the maxim "tout comprendre c'est tout pardonner." In a beautiful meditation he explains not only the relationship between error and truth, but also that between error and a lie: "Error is a belief that something untrue is true. A lie is a conscious distortion of truth. Error is noble and natural. A lie is unclean and human. Error is a lower degree of truth. A lie is an obstacle to truth. Error may be a great thing. A lie is low and ephemeral. Error elevates and stimulates. A lie debases and assassinates. Error is the heat which gives birth to the light of truth. A lie extinguishes the flame of truth. Only noble spirits can be in error. Only little men can lie."[40]

As could be expected, Knežević's conception of justice was tied to his idea of truth. "Justice is the result of the proportion of things."[41] Like truth, it reduces things to their proper limits, and the more precise these limits, the higher the justice.[42] Just as error is truth of a lower degree, evil is a good of a lower degree. "Evil is a narrow good, a good for just one man, one class, one people or time."[43] Thus, truth is essentially a righteous thought. The higher it is, the

---

[38] B. Knežević, *Zakon reda u istoriji,* p. 64.
[39] *Loc. cit.*
[40] B. Knežević, *Misli,* aphorism 602.
[41] B. Knežević, *Zakon reda u istoriji,* p. 63.
[42] *Loc. cit.*
[43] *Ibid.,* p. 62.

more beautiful it is, and the more it renders justice to an ever larger number of things.

But like his theory of truth, his doctrine of justice, of good and evil, does not provide an escape from the logical and moral dilemmas of relativism. In one instance he claims that "everything is good in its time and place"; in another that "the lack of freedom is always immoral and uneconomical."[44] Obviously, the moralist in Knežević prevailed at times over the logician. The conflict between the two was keen and could not be resolved even in the philosopher's assertion that "justice, like truth, is too great and sublime a principle to be seen in just one present, at one specific time, or in one particular place."[45] Almost religiously he relies on the belief that when one mankind matures completely, when it reaches that stage of its life which Löwith might call "the age of fulfilment," it will be able to understand that all things were necessary in their time and place, that all of them made sense, were true and justifiable as inevitable stepping-stones and crises of maturation. Again a secularized eschatological future is expected to redeem the past.

Closely related to Knežević's ideas of truth and justice is his concept of freedom. All three of them are logically rooted in his theory of the relationship between the whole and the part, on the one hand, and the parts with one another, on the other. He believes that the organization of things, implicit in the very process of evolution, leads to proportion. Organization is progress from disproportion to proportion.[46] Only when each thing occupies its proper place in space and time, "only when everything will have de-

---

[44] *Ibid.*, p. 70.
[45] *Ibid.*, pp. 63–4.
[46] B. Knežević, *Zakon reda u istoriji*, p. 58.

termined the proper limits of its size, duration, strength, and value, will come balance and peace, and the harmony of the whole."[47]

The other logical root of Knežević's idea of freedom lies in its Hegelian identification of unconsciousness with necessity and of consciousness with freedom. There is much more of the primordial condition of unconsciousness than there is of consciousness. "The same proportion of consciousness and unconsciousness that exists in an individual psyche, exists also in human society. No great phenomenon in history resulted from conscious human will. . . . Every invention and every discovery had unanticipated results, because it awakened new forces and uncovered new paths and tools in the great struggle of historical mankind. . . . The main spiritual achievements of humanity—religion, morality, language, art, and others—did not result from wilful, conscious activity of the human mind; instead, they emerged spontaneously as unconscious products of the natural movement and development of things."[48] Thus consciousness creates nothing. It only lights the way already travelled and the way that must be taken. In the history of mankind "consciousness awakened with the discovery of writing."[49]

As of all things reason is the weakest, as in every society men of reason constitute the smallest group, as, in fact, only a very small proportion of things can be understood, and as real freedom can be based only on consciousness and reason, it follows that "there is very little real freedom in the world, but a great deal of blind necessity, a great deal of the must."[50] The

[47] *Ibid.*, p. 59.
[48] B. Knežević, *Zakon proporcije u istoriji,* p. 154.
[49] B. Knežević, *Zakon reda u istoriji,* p. 24.
[50] B. Knežević, *Zakon proporcije u istoriji,* p. 154.

rule of the must extends over all the regions of the unconscious, and, as the unconscious embraces all the inorganic, the organic, and most of human life, the rule of the must covers all these fields. "Like consciousness and reason, freedom is only a tiny drop in the ocean of necessity; dependence is the most general fact of the universe."[51]

Applied to the realm of man, these reflections lead Knežević to the conclusion that "the large majority of men are merely unconscious and unwilling tools of nature, of their society, and their time," and that "real freedom and morality are still as rare among men as are justice and truth."[52] For man is free only when he acts independently of the pressure of his particular present, and of his narrow and selfish personal goals. "True morality can be found only in liberty; only a free man can be a moral person."[53] In an elaboration of these views Knežević adds that "the greater the reasoning power and the area of consciousness, the greater is the realm of freedom.... Freedom develops in history and with history.... Freedom of the will is nothing other than obedience to reason, which erupts with ever greater strength from the increasing depth of time."[54]

These speculations on consciousness and unconsciousness, freedom and necessity, recall to one's mind an entire series of prominent thinkers, from Spinoza, through Kant and Hegel, to Croce, Freud, and Jaspers. Obviously, Knežević was an eclectic and, as such, he belonged to many schools of thought, including certain aspects of positivism, evolutionism, historicism, Marxism and existentialism. It must be

[51] *Ibid.*, p. 155.
[52] *Loc. cit.*
[53] *Ibid.*, p. 156.
[54] *Loc. cit.*

emphasized, however, that eclecticism does not necessarily preclude the possibility of genuine originality.

At the pinnacle of evolution he sees the world as "one and only one whole." With impressive dialectical skill the whole is defined as follows: "After everything has taken its proper place in space and time, beside all other things, the life of the whole will begin. In order that the whole may exist, all the parts must be present; in order that all may be present, none must occupy the place of another; none must extend over its limits; in order to make a whole, there must be proportion. The whole is the result of proportion."[55]

Thus the philosopher insists that at the highest level of the history of mankind, all the elements of man's life, natural as well as historical, will be distributed and bound in such a way that none will predominate at the expense of the others, and that the general life of the entire organism will manifest itself only through the common and harmonious activity of all of them. "And only in that one, great organic whole can one arrive at complete morality, freedom, justice, and truth."[56]

Logically connected with this thought is his idea of peace, which "is nothing other than the regular, lawful, harmonious, and proportional movement of all the individual parts of the whole."[57] Such a dynamic peace can be achieved only in a united, mature mankind. In order to contribute to the realization of this ideal, Knežević imposes on history a definite moral task: "Now that astronomy has bound the earth to the cosmos, and biology the animals to the earth, and man to the animals, and psychology the soul of man to the soul of the animal, it remains for scientific his-

[55] B. Knežević, *Zakon reda u istoriji*, p. 60.
[56] *Ibid.*, p. 69.
[57] *Ibid.*, p. 60.

tory to bind man to man. . . . History is to bind all peoples and all times, to bring them closer to one another and to reconcile them. . . ."[58]

Knežević uses the term "history" sometimes as a reference to the life of mankind as a cosmic process and sometimes to designate the field of scholarship specializing in the study of that process. He also sees in history "the highest reason," "the highest criterion of Knowledge," the ultimate organization of all the sciences and the universal and final philosophy of the human intellect capable of reconciling all opposites and all contradictions. It is always clear from the context which of these meanings he has in mind.

Furthermore, he claims to see the signs that mankind is really developing according to his scheme. "All the artificial barriers with which egoism and unconsciousness have separated countries, peoples, religions, and epochs, are being destroyed. . . ."[59] The recurrent outbursts of the animal in man do not succeed in damping his hopes for mankind at the pinnacle of its development. "Man's need for mankind is still too high and too abstract a requirement to be generally realized. With the ever stronger feeling and need of humanity for itself, the notion of one mankind is beginning to ripen. Humanity emerges ever more visibly from behind the walls of nations, states, races, and tribes. All the factors of modern history are working for the creation of this one mankind, from ocean to press, from science and technology to the common needs of people; the need for one mankind is growing, and one mankind is ever more clearly coming into being."[60]

A comparison between his work and that of his suc-

[58] *Ibid.*, pp. 55, 57.
[59] *Loc. cit.*
[60] B. Knežević. *Zakon reda u istoriji*, p. 81.

cessors reveals that Knežević deserves a prominent place among the philosophers of history. Compare, for example, his quoted statements with the following passage from Jaspers: "The importance of the fact that the whole of mankind, that all the old cultures, have been drawn into this common stream of destruction or renewal has only become conscious during the last few decades. The older ones amongst us were, as children, still living entirely within the European consciousness."[61] "Today, for the first time there is a real unity of mankind which consists in the fact that nothing essential can happen anywhere that does not concern all."[62]

Knežević believes that the unification of peoples into an ever greater mankind is the result of the fundamental interest of man, his living conditions, and economy. Each people, as it progresses, needs all the others for its food and maintenance. "These well-understood common interests make for stronger and more permanent unity among men than any other forces."[63] It may be of interest again to compare these arguments with those of Karl Jaspers: "Motives on this passage to world unity are, for one thing, the will to power, which is no less alive today than at any other time, and which knows no bounds until it has subjugated everything, and, for another, amongst powers none of which dare risk a decision by force in view of the monstrous perils, the great planetary distress that presses toward agreement—and above both these, the idea of human solidarity."[64]

In a similar frame of mind Knežević remarks that "all the forces of modern history are working to

[61] K. Jaspers, *The Origin and Goal of History,* New Haven, 1953, p. 138.
[62] *Ibid.,* p. 139.
[63] B. Knežević, *Zakon reda u istoriji,* p. 55.
[64] K. Jaspers, *The Origin and Goal of History,* p. 196.

22

eradicate the national and tribal differences among peoples," that "one humanity will be at the end of the process which began with the human race," that "the historical process is only the evolution of the human species into man," and that "the great truth of man will survive all the little truths of tribes, peoples, and states."[65]

In the very beginning of his philosophy of history Božidar Knežević states that "all human struggles began with the struggle against nature," and that, as with the animals, it was first the struggle for the preservation of natural, physical life. "The struggle with nature is the basis of all man's other struggles, and of all social organization. In the course of progress this struggle is transposed more and more from nature to man himself and to society. Thus it was that, after the struggle with external nature, the internal, social struggle began—the struggle of man against man and against his animal nature. It follows, therefore, that culture, the triumph of man over nature, is much older than civilization, which is the triumph of man over the animal in himself."[66]

In a more extensive study it might be interesting to compare this distinction between culture and civilization with those of Spengler, Toynbee, and Schweitzer, as well as with current ideas of such anthropologists as Alfred Kroeber and Robert Redfield.

In a poetic sentence the Serbian philosopher asserts that "the attractive power of history, like that of the sun, is constantly growing; it increasingly attracts to itself all the dismembered parts of mankind and of its intellect, so that today primitive man is closer to civilized man than contemporary peoples were once

[65] B. Knežević, *Zakon reda u istoriji*, pp. 86, 91.
[66] *Ibid.*, p. 4.

to one another."[67] The history of mankind will reach a point in its development when progress in time will have attained its peak. This will be the delicate fulcrum of historical equilibrium, the zenith in the life of the earth.[68]

But even at the pinnacle of his historical maturity, man will not be able to penetrate the supreme mystery of his cosmic destiny: why he exists at all and why he has a history. Throughout his works Knežević repeats that man's task on earth is "to render justice to all things," but he does not even ask who will render justice to man himself. These ultimate questions the philosopher regards as unanswerable, because the entire universe, of which man's world is only a small, though to him a central part, is "but one word in the enormous book of time."[69] And how much can be understood from one word alone? Nothing.[70]

Following the moment of perfect harmony and proportion, of freedom, morality, peace, and understanding, things-in-general, and man first of all will begin their slow and implacable return to the unconsciousness of primordial chaos.[71] "For not only do things come into being whenever they become necessary, but they last only as long as they are necessary; as soon as they are no longer needed, they disappear."[72] And as, in Knežević's scheme, the total span of time available to the living whole is determined and limited, the later a particular phenomenon arises, the less time there remains to it to exist; the later the necessity for a thing arises, the less time it lasts, the

[67] *Ibid.*, p. 57.
[68] B. Knežević, *Red u istoriji,* Belgrade, 1898, p. 300.
[69] *Ibid.*, p. 302.
[70] *Loc. cit.*
[71] *Ibid.*, p. 299.
[72] B. Knežević, *Zakon reda u istoriji*, p. 83.

sooner it disappears. "The succession of disappearances is reciprocal to that of appearances. . . . The prior survives the posterior."[73] Man is more ancient than races, tribes, and peoples, and he will survive them. "The psychic, as a later development, is the first to return to the organic; later the organic returns to the inorganic, and the inorganic, as the life of the whole, survives both"[74]

Religion is the original source of all the divisions and branches of the human spirit, whose historical progress tends towards the dissolution of all its particular forms in one common religion, which will absorb all particular laws, philosophies, sciences, and denominations. "The last task of philosophical history will be to work out a rational system of religion."[75] This should be a religion of civilization, humaneness, and man, based on faith in the power of nature and of the human mind. "Belief lies at the basis of all knowledge, and belief becomes the end of all knowledge; belief is everything to man; all things originate in it, and all return to it; it precedes everything and will survive everything."[76] In continuation of the same train of thought Knežević adds that "ultimately belief absorbs all knowledge, for less and less time is available for verifying all the processes, methods, and proofs by which one comes to understand the results of research. More and more one can believe only in the results of science."[77]

These and other reflections of Knežević on faith and religion deserve a systematic comparison with similar speculations in Jaspers, as well as with Speng-

[73] *Loc. cit.*
[74] *Ibid.,* p. 86.
[75] B. Knežević, *Red u istoriji,* p. 283, 284.
[76] B. Knežević, *Zakon reda u istoriji,* p. 88.
[77] *Ibid.,* p. 87.

ler's predictions on the "second religiosity" and credulity of the masses.

Although completely alien to all dogmatic theology, Knežević made an interesting attempt at defining the Supreme Being in purely rationalistic terms. With an almost Spinozist regularity and geometry he proposes the following definition of God: "As the earlier is more lasting and greater, more independent and necessary, more general and mighty, deeper and more regular, that which is the earliest, which pre-exists everything else, is in all times, remains after everything else, is only one, occupies all spaces, is always and everywhere, is itself perfect regularity and harmony, is eternal, permanent, unchanging; it is the essence itself; it exists by itself alone, creates everything else, is the cause and condition of itself, is needed by everything later, but does not need anything itself, it is self-sufficient; everything later depends upon it, whereas it does not depend on anything else; it maintains itself only by itself, from within itself; it creates everything and destroys everything; it is the absolute, it is the perfect truth, the highest reason; it understands everything, nothing can be understood without it! That Earliest is and only can be God!"[78]

At the time of man's entrance into history, nature affected him by its externals: "Civilizations first appeared in those regions where external nature was convenient to them. . . . With the ever continuing progress, all man's acquisitions, his religious and philosophical ideas, depend less and less on external nature, and more and more on its internal life (coal, sun, etc.)."

In his belief in the increasing importance of the sun

[78] B. Knežević, *Zakon proporcije u istoriji*, p. 171.

for the future of mankind Knežević goes so far as to predict that "the cult of the Sun will mark the end of conscious science just as it marked the beginning of unconscious religion."[79]

As "law tends to become custom, and conscious action mechanical," so again "the sciences are becoming arts and crafts as they were in the beginning."[80] Before Spengler, Knežević predicts that "art and craft will survive philosophy and science. The traces of man's craft are the oldest monuments of his life, and they will be his last relics too."[81]

Like man himself, his civilization has wandered until now from region to region; various centers were its prototypes; Memphis and Thebes; Babylon and Nineveh; Athens and Rome; Byzantium and Córdoba; Paris and London. "Wandering, the civilization of mankind is coming closer and closer to its real center, which cannot be anywhere in space—in any one city, at any one point on the globe. The real center of mankind and its history can be but in time: it can be only an idea."[82]

Knežević's philosophy of history ends in an apocalyptic vision of general dying which begins with man: "Since the light of civilization appears first on the peaks of society in individual elevated minds, and only then descends into the depths and valleys, it follows from the law of disappearance that civilization and progress will start dying out in the masses of society, where they penetrated last, and that in the end education and civilization will remain only on the peaks, in the minds of elevated individuals, from which they descended in the beginning. The peaks of

[79] B. Knežević, *Zakon reda u istoriji,* pp. 84, 89.
[80] *Ibid.,* p. 90.
[81] *Loc. cit.*
[82] B. Knežević, *Misli,* aphorism 390.

27

mankind will still flame in the sunset when darkness and ignorance shall have long since overwhelmed the masses. As the sunlight disappears first from the lowlands, while the mountain peaks still glisten in the light of the setting sun, so when peoples fall, it is only the individual spirits that continue to bear the standard of national ideals; they alone remain the bearers of its history. The light of history still illumines the elevated minds long after it has left the deeps and valleys of society. . . . Accordingly, the light of civilization, of consciousness and reason, was born on the eminences of society, and there it will be extinguished last."[83]

Man and his civilization, his spiritual life and progress are, to Knežević, merely "the luxuries of nature." "When the earth's energy begins to diminish, when it becomes necessary to concentrate the disappearing resources at her command, the spiritual life of man and man's civilization will be sacrificed first, as man himself, in his emergences, jettisons first of all his own spiritual life. The natural man, with his natural needs, will long survive civilization and history, these luxuries of his long existence."[84] "Mankind will die in savagery and darkness as it was born in savagery and darkness."[85]

Thus, everything which appeared in time will disappear in time; "all things born must die. Only what never began will never end; what preceded everything else will survive everything else; what appeared first will disappear last."[86]

His vision of the end is reminiscent of an equally disturbing premonition of Jaspers, who refers to the

[83] B. Knežević, *Zakon reda u istoriji*, pp. 91, 92.
[84] *Loc. cit.*
[85] *Ibid.*, p. 85.
[86] *Ibid.*, p. 92.

beginning and the end of history in the following words: "This leap made by humanity which resulted in history may be conceived of as a disaster that overtook mankind; something incomprehensible happened; the fall of man, the intrusion of an alien power: history is a process of annihilation in the cycle of a firework that may be magnificent but is short-lived; that which took place at the outset may be reversed again; in the end man will return to the blissful state of his prehistoric existence."[87]

We may console ourselves with the hope that, as both of these gloomy premonitions pertain of necessity to something that has not yet happened, their ominous implicatons need never be fulfilled. But at the outset of the atomic age, in a confused and troubled world, we can hardly afford to dismiss them as utterly fantastic and impossible.

According to George Gaylord Simpson, "Continuity of basic physical conditions may persist for many millions of years or may end tomorrow. It is incredible that it should really continue forever. The sun's energy is finite and must someday reach an end and with it life on the earth must cease. Collision with other celestial bodies, extremely improbable in such limited time as man conceives, is eventually probable in the endless time of 'forever.' Man himself seems terrifyingly near the knowledge of how to destroy his planet in a blazing chain reaction, and terrifyingly far from the self-control necessary to avoid using this knowledge.

"It must be concluded that material racial immortality is impossible. The time will come when all life ends. The fantasy of transfer to other planets is not

[87] K. Jaspers, *The Origin and Goal of History*, p. 47.

impossible although it is hardly imminent. This might postpone but could not avoid the inevitable end."[88]

Knežević's basic idea is therefore scientifically plausible.

In his *History as the Story of Liberty* Benedetto Croce speaks of the confusion of concept and imagination as the essential constructive principle of myths. "This mythological character of philosophies of history is self-evident. They all want to discover and reveal the Weltplan, the design of the world from its birth to its death, or from its entry into time to its entry into eternity. . . ."[89]

Like so many other philosophers of history, Knežević could not resist the temptation to indulge in myth-making and prophecy. But his cosmic orientation, despite its frank determinism and teleology, did not lead him into dogmatism. Unlike Hegel and many of his followers, Knežević did not believe in the finality and absolute validity of his own system. He did not overlook that, on its own premises, his work was bound to be superseded and subjected to critical reinterpretations by posterity, to the judgment of time, which is, after all, the highest criterion of knowledge accessible to man.[90] In a moving image he expresses his awareness of the inevitable limitations of his own theories by comparing all systems of philosophy to perishable palaces from whose debris grow new structures of thought.

Space does not permit us to go any further. The specific terms of Knežević's acquaintance with and indebtedness to his predecessors and contemporaries; the exact degree and kind of stimulation and influence he received from particular schools of thought,

[88] G. G. Simpson, *The Meaning of Evolution* (1952), pp. 195–6.
[89] B. Croce, *History as the Story of Liberty*, p. 142.
[90] B. Knežević, *Zakon reda u istoriji*, p. 62.

books, and personalities; the ideas and theories in which he clearly anticipates some of his famous successors; the merits and shortcomings of his literary style and of the entire poetic conception of his major works; and, finally, touching the problem of his originality, the principles of selection underlying his highly personal eclecticism—these are only a few of the many interesting questions that remain to be discussed in a definitive study, which this long-neglected man and philosopher eminently deserves.

PART I

THE LAW OF SUCCESSION IN HISTORY

One of the basic laws of natural and human history is *the law* of succession. The succession of events in the natural world and in the process of individual and social development is identical; the progress of matter and the progress of mind and spirit proceed in the same order.

CHAPTER I

Nature is prior to man, and all that is natural precedes the human and the humane. Nature was completed in all its important aspects when man appeared; he arrived at a far advanced moment of cosmic development, and for this reason we assert the priority of nature.

The natural origin of man is much more ancient than his humane origin, that is, than the origin of his culture and civilization. Man as an animal species antedates by far man, the social animal. His historical, social groupings began, at the most, some tens of thousands of years ago, while his animal origin fades away into the remote, natural, brute darkness.

Before man's spiritual progress could begin, his natural, physical organization had to be perfected, and *nature had to progress to the extent that man could appear and develop in it at all.*

All human struggles began with the struggle against nature, and, as with the animals, it was first the struggle for the preservation of natural, physical life. The struggle with nature is the basis of all man's other struggles, and of all social organization. In the course of progress this conflict is transposed more and more from nature to man himself and to society. Thus it was that, after the struggle with external nature, the internal, social struggle began, the struggle of man against man and against his animal nature. It follows, therefore, that culture, the triumph of man over nature, is much older than civilization, which is the triumph of the humane in man over the animal within himself.

The first human society was a natural society—the family, a grouping which also exists among animals. At first, the family was a purely natural relationship; only later did it gradually acquire its humane and moral character, as it took over the task of moral education and preparation for participation in society. The family is the first purely natural basis on which were later erected the higher, historical forms of human society.

Primordial man is only a natural man. He possesses only what nature gives him, goes only where she leads him; he feels and thinks only at the direct stimulation from external nature.

The first diversification of mankind was into races, and the racial varieties result from the action of external nature rather than of human history. The dissimilarities among the races are physical, natural. The first differences among peoples were natural. The historical and social differences arose later.

The first subjects of history, after the natural age of man, were the peoples who were composed and grouped by external natural influences and conditions. And thus it has happened that lands have first had their histories, and only then the nations.

Nature preconditions the production and distribution of wealth, and natural economy forms the first phase of all economic history.

The first foundations of the historical life of man were laid down only in those regions where nature gave him all he needed for living and for developing. Civilization's basic requirements are natural; the historical requirements arise only later. Warmth, the first basic necessity for all organic development, was the primary condition for civilization; the first civilizations could only appear in warm countries and along fertile rivers. These civilizations were natural in that they were based not on history, but on nature; the historical civilizations arose only later.

Accordingly, the free states of modern society are more and more frequently founded on the principles of humaneness and justice, while the early civilizations were based on the purely natural, brutal right of the stronger.

Not only the appearance of mankind, but also its movement over the face of the earth and the development of its cultures were determined originally by nature. Having established the first civilizations in the east and south, the ancient man had to migrate farther and farther to the west and north, under the pressure of overpopulation and the lack of food. It was only in those regions where nature was harsh and where man, therefore, had to depend most on his own efforts, that the value of and the respect for labor and everything humane came about, through man's emancipation from, and elevation above, natural conditions.

The notion of *natural right* was more strongly developed among the original peoples than it is today; the idea of *historical right* began to develop only in modern nations, because the influence of time and history is much greater now than it was among the ancient peoples, overwhelmed as they were by nature.

The first religion was natural and direct. The religion of primitive men and of all pre-Christian peoples consisted in the worship of natural forces and phenomena; all religion was at first but a cult of nature. The awakened moral consciousness, searching for that which is ethical in religion, appeared much later.

As the pressure and the supremacy of external nature became weaker and weaker, religion became more and more humane and inward; the more nature, through knowledge, became subject to man, the milder it became. The worship of blind and ruthless natural forces gradually passed over into the worship of good and evil spirits, who were believed to determine human destiny. It was with the greater mastery of nature by man that the worship of the idealized and humane became stronger. Thus, the destiny of man rested at first on the will of harsh and jealous gods; the idea that man makes his own destiny appeared only later. All the religious festivals before Christ were purely natural; they were founded upon the succession of celestial phenomena and the seasons.

Buddhism and Christianity are the first historical, ethical and humane religions to appear after the primitive, natural ones. In both of these religions the ethical and humane prevail over the natural. With Buddha and Christ religion began to be inspired by man and no longer by nature.

The same course of events occurred in art. Architecture developed as the first of all the arts, because it is closest to nature, whose products are themselves largely architectural. Thus, man first pictured natural objects; the imitation of nature in painting developed not only among natural but among civilized ancient peoples as well, while the representation of man is a later development. Likewise, in music, rhythm, the most elemental and natural component, appeared first. Similarly, the first intimation of the tragic came from the feeling of an external destiny arising in nature, outside and above the self. The conception that man carries his own fate in himself and prepares it for himself came only later.

Nature was the first school of man, and the first subject of his questions and studies; the contemplation and study of man and of society followed after. Thus, the study of nature and natural laws has already arisen to the level of science, while in the field of the humanities precise laws still await discovery. Lamarck and Darwin could destroy the anthropocentric error, *the error of man about man,* only after Copernicus had destroyed the geocentric error, *the error of man about nature.* The earth had first to be taken from her prevailing, unnatural position and made a part of a great whole; only afterwards could the same be done with man!

CHAPTER II

The material, real and physical precedes the
non-material and spiritual; nature evolves into
increasingly purer and more ideal forms.

Man's first struggles were the physical, sentient,
purely animal struggles for food and life. Throughout antiquity wars were political and economic. The
new form of struggle—the religious conflict, the fight
for inner convictions—arose only later.

The physical and economic life of peoples had, first
of all, to be sufficiently advanced before the political
and social life of the people could arise upon it as
upon a foundation. And of all social theories, political
economy, the theory of the material, physical life of
mankind, was the first to appear. The primitive age of
man can be considered the "body" of history, in which
and from which, in the course of time, developed the
historical "soul" of mankind which awakened in the
first civilization.

Early peoples created only material cultures; all the
ancient civilizations were more or less material and
sentient; they were more cultures of *nature* than of
man. True civilization, the culture of soul and spirit,
could come only when the sentient, physical life was
assured.

The human spirit first perceives and comprehends
the material; sense impressions are the matter out of

which later develop higher forms of mental life. Sensations are the first material of mental life. And every new knowledge appears first in the form of feeling; it is here that the great truths are always born; every idea has been anticipated in feeling long before it receives its pure form in the mind of an individual thinker, and a still longer period elapses before it becomes the common good of mankind. Accordingly, real, material objects are the first content of consciousness and thinking. Originally, our perceptions are of the real objects themselves; it is thought that stimulates and leads our consciousness to abstractions. So it is that words presently applied to abstractions had originally a concrete meaning, as the material and sensible prevails in the beginning in every language.

The first money was directly valuable in itself—it had use value—livestock, skins and the like were the first currency, and they had, of course, a much greater value than the later forms.

Originally, man thought in terms of images of real objects. Just as the original words were spoken pictures of the things themselves, the first writings were written pictures, and, similarly, the early currencies were equal to the direct values of the objects they represented. The Egyptians were the first to create definite characters from the multitude of pictured objects. Peoples and tribes first wrote their histories in real objects—temples, palaces, pyramids, and other monuments.

Law existed long before laws were written down; language existed before written grammar; beauty was created long before the first esthetics; peoples survived events and made history long before recorded history. Things existed long before they got their names, because they existed long before man began to think of them. Natural sciences existed in their respective areas long before the modern age gave them their names.

In religion, also, real objects—animals, trees, rivers, celestial bodies and other phenomena—were the first deities. In the course of progress religion sloughed off more and more of the material, sensual elements and lifted itself toward purer forms.

Likewise, the deed, the act, is prior to the thought about it. The original history of every people lies in its deeds, and the phenomena that first attract historical interest are felt things, especially wars, because they require the exertion of the greatest physical efforts.

Consequently, the rise from the real and material toward the ever more ideal and non-material is one of the aspects of human progress; the lower the mind, the more deeply it is sunk into reality, the more it thinks and speaks only of material affairs and concrete things, and the more necessary reality is for it.

In a similar way practice preceded theory.

All the sciences developed from practical experience, and from the needs of everyday life. Astronomy developed from the practical need for the division of time and for accurate orientation in space and time. Geometry was born of the practical need for measuring land. Practical mechanics was known to the most primitive peoples, although ages elapsed before an Archimedes developed theoretical mechanics. Chemistry developed largely from metallurgy, whose useful elementary principles were known from the earliest time. Commerce and travel paved the way for geography. Botany developed from the search for

42

edible and medicinal plants. A practical knowledge of anatomy existed long before the theoretical. Medicine developed from the practical need for curing the ill. History was first written from a practical point of view—for instruction and example—because it was considered to be the teacher of life.

Thus, every science began as a practical skill; skill or special ability is the basis of every science. Astrology, the art of reading human destiny from the stars, was the first phase of astronomy; chemistry's first period was alchemy, the secret and sacred art of changing base metals to gold and of preparing the elixir of life; botany began with the ability to distinguish poisonous plants from edible and medical species; history was the art of deriving useful lessons for the future from the events of the past.

The first philosophers held the view that the primary and ultimate substance of all things is material; in early Greek philosophy it was successively maintained to be water, then fire, then air. Only later did the primordial substance come to be conceived more abstractly and the soul to be thought of in a less material way.

Certain material fluids were the first principles of physics, the first explanations of particular physical states, forces and phenomena. Light was believed to be a certain kind of matter emanating from shining bodies; heat was conceived as a specific kind of matter; electricity and magnetism were understood as special sorts of fluids; and all nature was held to be composed of specific kinds of material elements.

It follows, naturally, that the doctrine of the conservation of matter preceded that of the conservation of energy.

Similarly, the personalities of great men are even now considered by some to be the only creative factor in history. The original concept of the soul was likewise materialistic; the soul was first imagined as a substantial being inhabiting the body.

CHAPTER III

Thus, the human spirit evolves from the sensual and concrete toward the ideal and abstract. There is a continually diminishing material content in things and phenomena.

Originally, sensory activity and imagination filled and endowed all of nature with a spiritual content, which a better, maturer understanding later eliminated. At first, matter was thought to be live and animate; only a later view of the world brought about the interpretation of nature in terms of mechanical laws. The primitive mind saw inner life everywhere; later the concept of life came to be replaced by that of energy. Thus, the phenomena of plants and animals used to be explained as due to some special life-giving forces. Only later did it become clear that nature contains no such special forces.

The original, almost exlusive, dependence upon physical strength led to the cult of force. The heroes of early mankind were strong men who physically struggled against evils. But, while strength was the basis of the first aristocracies in all historical societies, it contained also the germ of moral strength *(vis, vir, virtus)*. In the history of man the rule of force is far older than the reign of duty; the moral idea grew from the concept of power. The first right was the right of the stronger.

The history of mankind has been created, thus far,

only by the strong and powerful. Formerly it was, in fact, merely an apology of force and power; but now, like religion, it is turning its attention to the common man.

In physiology, the first hypothesis was that of a *vital principle* according to which life is a force separate and distinct from the properties of matter.

Likewise, weight was considered a definite entity in bodies, and electricity and magnetism also. Even intellectual and moral abstractions were considered to have the nature of vital principles.

Thus, the laws and causes by which we explain things now stand toward these vital forces as our contemporary alphabet stands toward the picture writing of earlier man.

Natural religions were, in the beginning, full of life; they were living poetry. Later they were reduced to formal dogmatics; the cult of vital forces was replaced by that of abstract dogmas, and, during this process, prayer lost the content which once filled it with life and practical value.

Originally, all human actions were full of life and meaning; every action grew out of a living belief, each was a part of the cult of good and evil spirits. Today, actions are deprived of life and meaning, like today's dead words and alphabets. Thus, the dance was originally an act of worship, an expression of homage to the deities; then it was still a living and significant action; today, from an important religious activity, dancing has become but an amusement. So the serious struggles, the victories and triumphs of old, became in social games the entertainments of the present.

Like words, letters, and customs, proverbs were once living things also; they encompassed the entire story of an event; only later were they subjugated to moral instruction and reduced to the naked sentence.

Before words appeared the only expressions were the live motions of hands, face, and body. The first words were intended to imitate an object; to picture the being who was performing an action. They were a part of the thing itself; from this arose the belief in the internal value and content of the word and the superstition in curing by spells. But today words are only naked forms and skeletons.

CHAPTER IV

This first content of things and phenomena, this internal vitalism, was imagined as live, personal beings and their actions. Childish and primitive minds always try to explain phenomena as results of personal activities; it is the task of the mature intellect to reduce the means of explanation to more and more impersonal and abstract laws, by eliminating the personal from things and phenomena. This constitutes the succession from the personal to the impersonal.

In the beginning, man takes himself as the measure of all things; he studies and considers all things in relation to himself, and judges everything by himself. All that occurs is a result of motives like his own; this explains why personality is found behind all natural phenomena. As religion develops, in place of the cult of living forces and personalities, progressively impersonal, dogmatic cults appear. The more advanced a religion, the less it contains of living beings and personal wills.

The first Greek philosophies consisted in the elimination of the personal from nature; instead of gods of fire and water, fire and water became independent forces. Previously, the electrical energy in amber and the attractive power of the lodestone had been ascribed to some souls in them. The first discovered gases, including the air, were conceived as spiritual beings (*geist,* gas, *spiritus, vazduh*), and diseases as evil spirits which gained entrance to the body.

Now science itself is becoming more and more the product of an impersonal, historical spirit. The personality and individuality of the thinker and discoverer fade more and more into the historical continuity, his work bears less and less the stamp of his personality; instead, it becomes ever more the result of the past, of history, and of abstract historical laws.

At first the entire body of history itself consisted only of stories about individuals; the histories of epochs and peoples were concentrated in accounts of individual personalities, and individual histories, in the biography of a mighty hero, incidental to the description of his life and deeds. The undeveloped historical consciousness considered personality as the prime mover, the initiative of the hero as the creator of an event, and ignored the long chain of preparations, struggles and conditions which called the event into being. So history was first the history of personalities; only later could it become the history of ideas. The growing understanding of history enables us to see that all great men are only the products of the conditions of their times, that they are great only in relation to their age, and that all human greatness is conditioned by history, by the past and present, by social environment. Personalities are ever more clearly recognized as instruments of history, deriving their significance from their relation to many other persons, both before and after them.

Thus, the less developed a society, the greater is the strength and influence of individuals, the more they are the only carriers of all events and developments.

Forceful personalities are the first points of social crystallization; it is through them that peoples are linked to their destiny. Some tribes even receive their names from their great leaders; the early folk poetry incarnated the traits of entire peoples in the personalities of their leaders. In those times individuals served in place of institutions; men were the important element in society. Whole eras were dated by the lives of great individuals; minstrels and bards were the guardians of the precious memories of national life and history.

Whenever an institution is attacked, it is first of all the persons who are denounced and then the system itself. The struggle against personalities is always the first phase of the struggle against a system. The conflict of the awakened spirit against religion starts as a revolt against the persons of popes and priests. In the first Greek comedy it was contemporary personalities who were ridiculed; only later did authors begin to satirize institutions and society itself. Likewise, the ruler no longer rules the people but [more impersonally] the state.

CHAPTER V

Whatever is direct precedes the indirect, for directness is the characteristic of the senses, and of the sensual view of life.

Man's relations with nature are in the beginning direct; his first preoccupation with nature is concerned with the immediate satisfaction of his needs; his early knowledge is derived from the immediate perception of his environment, and the first stages of mental life are constructed from direct sensory impressions. The primitive idea that certain characteristics of things directly inhabit all their parts, and the belief that the soul inhabits all parts of the body gave rise to the faith in religious relics.

The mind of primordial man, as well as that of the child and the animal, is guided and determined directly by the physical; their souls are in an immediate relation with their bodies; their perceptions and presentments are in instant connection with the objects of reality. Feeling is the primordial form of all mental life; it is a direct function of the psyche. In the sense of touch, which develops before all the other senses, stimulation is more direct than in other, later senses.

The lower the forms of life, the more direct is their link with nature. Plants and animals are more closely bound to nature than is man, and they live the life of the earth more than he does. This is why animals feel and anticipate more directly the changes and stresses in nature, while man's link with the earth is far more distant. His emotions, being the more primitive, the lower and deeper forces of his soul, are more closely connected not only with the world, but with his body as well, more at least than are his thoughts and presentments. In the later development of man the soul becomes progressively less interwoven with the body. And as a more mature mankind frees its civilization, little by little, from direct influences of nature, so the spirit of man frees itself from the immediate influence of his physical environment. The ideas of Jesus, of Newton and Darwin, were not directly conditioned by external circumstances of nature, but were the fruits of the entire human history. In these cases personalities were only the tools of history.

In the beginning man's emotions and presentments are linked with the immediate present. Originally, the sciences studied things in their present, until the need for better understanding required a knowledge of their past and future. A knowledge of history becomes increasingly indispensable for the highest understanding of all things.

The first languages were direct explanations by means of gestures, mimicry, and interjections; the first characters were pictures of the objects themselves; they were written interjections.

At the lowest level of religious development the sacred object is directly deified; the god is in the phenomenon itself. Deity appears to primitive man in direct pronouncements, or in direct intervention in natural events and in human destiny; hence the ancient belief in the immanence of gods and in their interference with human affairs. Religion first looked for direct links between man and gods; later, philosophy linked god with man only through the continued mediation of many other, earlier phenomena. Religious faith is an immediate, spontaneous faith, for which the human soul needs no instruction and education: the philosophical, scientific faith is not immediate; it develops only indirectly as a result of many prior conditions and forces.

The belief that all that exists is only for the benefit of man derives from the primitive belief in the direct interference of deities in human affairs. Hence, man formerly related all natural phenomena to himself, because, originally, he was the center of all things. The belief of every ancient people that it alone was the chosen of God, and the more modern view that man, the most intelligent of all creatures, is the natural ruler of the rest of nature—that only he is endlessly perfectible and that his spirit alone is immortal—are only consequences of the primitive belief that man is the center of all things.

Every preliminary study begins with a direct examination of phenomena. Geocentrics is the result of a direct, sensual vision of the world. It was believed at first that certain characteristics and forces of the soul are directly related to specific organs. The earlier the level of development of a science, the more occupied it is with immediately present objects and phenomena.

The beginnings of all progress and all civilizations were influenced directly by nature. The basis of man's historical life existed only in regions where nature presented to him directly all that he needed for his development. The first relationships among persons were blood ties, direct, intimate and limited. The first money was an immediately valuable thing itself. Architecture, the most directly useful art, developed before all the others. Direct and immediate usefulness was the primary stimulus of every study, and the first phase of every science. *Medicine,* one of the most directly useful sciences, was scholarship's most ancient stimulus, and knowledge of nature was first the possession of those who treated the sick. Chemistry and botany, anatomy and physiology, were merely the servants of medicine. Astrology was the first phase of astronomy, a phase when the stars and the phenomena of the sky were observed and studied only with regard to man. Alchemists, searching for the elixir of life and for gold, provided the basis for the chemistry which was to follow. Phrenology, seeking direct benefits from the knowledge of the physiological structure of the skull and brain, developed before physiology.

Commerce and wars, the quest for gains and benefits in remote countries, first paved the way for traffic and for a knowledge of geography. Likewise, Columbus undertook his voyage not to discover America or to complete knowledge about the earth, but to resolve a commerical difficulty, to find a shorter seaway to India, the land of gold and jewels.

The search for direct, immediate usefulness was the first phase of history. The trials and errors of previous generations were preserved for the example and instructions of the later ones. Even among modern nations, history was for long a mere servant of ethics, which used it merely as a source of examples and exhortation. The fact that the sciences, especially the practical ones, developed first, caused the need for scientific history and the more purely intellectual activities to be felt only later.

It was only when increasing population increased human needs to such an extent that they could no longer be directly satisfied by nature but could be satisfied only through human labor that men found in their labor the best and sturdiest foundation for their civilization. From being only a consumer, man became a producer. Similarly, the first period of life of every individual human being is entirely consumptive. The consuming classes of peoples and of societies have heretofore been the only subjects of history, as history was interested only in consumers, while the productive masses, the lower classes, only recently became objects of historical study.

CHAPTER VI

*The arts develop before the sciences, since the
real and sensible precedes the ideal and abstract.*

The arts, having fewer obstacles and more stimuli
to their development than sciences and philosophies,
develop before the latter. They pave the way, they
prepare the ground for all the further development
and education of the human spirit; epochs of art precede epochs of science. Every truth appears first in
the form of beauty. Mathematics was first studied in
architecture, anatomy in painting; drama contained
the first moral philosophy; the epic gave birth to history, the science of sounds developed for the sake of
music; it was Pythagoras who first demonstrated the
elements of harmony. The belief that the earth is
round was first based on esthetic reasons
(Pythagoras). The Universe is first the Cosmos.

Poetry is the first fruit of the developing human
spirit. The natural language of the most primitive
peoples, it was the first step in the entire spiritual life
of man. Among all the ancient and classical peoples,
and in the beginning stages of the development of
modern nations, all the cultural and educational resources were found in poetry. Poetry stimulated
them, and poetry developed from them. One people
influences another primarily through its art.

Since popular ideas are conceived in popular

poetry, since it is their primary medium, ideas always penetrate the people first through poetry. Poets were the first to pave the way for great ideas; they were their first protagonists. Poets are the first investigators of the human soul. It is the poets who first elaborate and refine the primitive religious myths and thereby present much material to science and philosophy. Among the Greeks it was first the poets who abandoned the popular faith, then the philosophers. Folk poetry was the chief means of expression of public opinion until the XVI century. Poets everywhere were the first creators of languages; languages appear and grow with poetry; it is the cradle of all the literary languages; it is always the first form of literature. Only when history was separated from the epic did prose separate from poetry.

Thus, that which is beautiful clears the way to every good of mankind—to freedom, to justice, to truth.

The beautiful precedes the useful. As the child "feels" and desires that which is beautiful before it can know what is useful to him, and what harmful, so does man rejoice in the beautiful before he notices the useful. All the metals were first used as ornaments; gold, silver, bronze, and iron were made into decorations and jewelry before they were applied to practical, useful purposes. Man made ornaments before he made garments. Clothing developed from ornamentation; there are peoples without clothing, but there are none without ornaments. The first traders dealt in luxury articles—precious metals, pearls, jewels, expensive materials.

CHAPTER VII

*Likewise, the sensual presentment of space
precedes the abstract concept of time.*

The laws of space were discovered before all the others. The first sciences were concerned with spatial laws and relations. The knowledge of spatial phenomena was the first to rise to the level of science. The great primary task of astronomy was to establish the spatial relationship of the celestial bodies, and astronomy was the first independent science, the first among all the natural sciences to reach complete exactness. It was the first to free itself from the bondage of usefulness and of religion; thus it prepared the way and served as an example for the other sciences. Copernicus discovered the relationships of the earth *in space* before Newton could ascertain the laws of her movement *in time*. Again, according to the same law of succession, the theory of gravitation is older than the theory of evolution. By gravitation one can explain the relations of the celestial bodies in space, by evolution one interprets the temporal relations of things, i.e., their development in time. Geography, which studies the earth's surface and man's relationship to it, in space, is a more ancient science than history, which concerns itself with man in time.

In language, also, all the notions of time were originally those of space. The words "past," "present," "future" had, in the beginning, only a spatial reference.

Works of architecture are most intimately related to space; and [of all man's works] occupy the most space; the laws of the science of space are the laws of architecture. Only in music and in poetry did the spirit of the artists free itself from all spatial relations.

The prior importance of space is more and more evident, the more deeply one penetrates into the life of natural man and of nature in general; nomadic cattle-raisers need much more space than civilized man does. It was civilization that developed the need for and the value of time.

CHAPTER VIII

Since things come into being unconsciously be-
fore man thinks of them and understands them,
since everything in nature and in man is origi-
nally unconscious, the unconscious always pre-
cedes the conscious.

1. Whatever was created, was created only in the darkness of unconsciousness. Consciousness creates nothing. It only lights the way already traveled and the way that is to be taken. All the greatest achievements of mankind—religion, morality, language, art, law, the state—are not products of a conscious human will, of a conscious activity of mind; instead, they emerged spontaneously, from the depth of human nature, as results of the unconscious historical life of mankind.

2. Unconscious instinct was the first stimulus and the initial step toward all knowledge: Every discovery, every new truth was prepared unconsciously, and happened unintentionally, and unwillingly. It is for this reason that, from a superficial point of view, they appear accidental. Emotion always precedes ideas; the first phase of the idea is feeling and anticipation. Many minds unconsciously clear the way for each truth long before it bursts into human consciousness. Quite unconsciously, the astrologers created astronomy, as the alchemists brought chemistry into being. All the great inventions and discoveries in his-

tory, from that of fire to that of America and further, came unconsciously. Man either stumbles in the darkness upon something new and unknown, or he looks for one thing only to find something quite different, which he neither knew of nor expected. (While searching for gold, the alchemists discovered many chemical truths and laws; while seeking a shorter route to the Indies, Columbus stumbled upon America.)

The fact that in the course of history everything appears without conscious effort; the fact that over enormous periods of time human consciousness and will are reduced to a minimum; the fact that the history of mankind follows its course independently of the conscious will of man—only go to prove that the historical process develops according to unchanging and predetermined laws; that all which has appeared, which was discovered and found in history, came because it had to come, and at the time it had to come, without the will and consciousness of man.

In the history of mankind consciousness awakened with the discovery of writing, for mankind could transmit its heritage to succeeding generations only by means of writing.

Accordingly, all the sciences developed as unintentional and unexpected results of life and experience. The first results of astronomy were unintentional and unplanned. They came about as a by-product of observations whose original purpose was not to enlarge the horizon of human knowledge and understanding by the determination of the constellations, but to predict human destiny; yet all this helped, unintentionally and unpurposefully, the astronomical science which was to follow.

CHAPTER IX

As all differences are only particular forms and parts developed from an original, uniform general condition, we may conclude that simplicity and uniformity always precede complexity and diversity.

The more primitive a body, the simpler it is, the more its parts resemble one another. The earlier and less developed a body, the more it resembles its environment, and the more passively it participates in changes in environment. At the time of conception every organism, even the highest, does not differ at all from other organisms in their embryonic state.

Originally, mankind was one and homogeneous; there were no racial differences; moreover, the differences among tribes and peoples developed only after differences in race developed. For, at the primary stage of human life, the course of development is everywhere the same; all men of all tribes, peoples, and races of all times pass through the same phase at the beginnings of life; differences arise in later and higher phases. Even the beginnings of civilization were always and everywhere the same.

For man first inhabited regions of mild and unvaried climate, without much difference in seasons and in temperatures; only later did he migrate to regions with alternating seasons.

Religion also has the same origins everywhere. Fetishism was everywhere and always basically the same, and fetishes are always the same—the same natural phenomena are always personified and worshiped. Only when monotheism developed did real religious differences appear. Moreover, the differences among religions are, in substance, much less important than those occurring in the later developed scientific and philosophic ideas.

CHAPTER X

Since later variations are only forms and parts which developed from the primordial, unvaried, general stage of things, the undifferentiated precedes the specific; the particular develops from the universal.

In nature, a common stage precedes various specific forms and phenomena. *Instinct,* for example, is a general force, common to men and animals; it is *the first form of faith.* Religion—belief in the good and evil forces of nature and in their power over men—is a more specialized form of this faith, which does not occur in animals. Religion is a common disposition of the human spirit, shared by all men everywhere, and at all times. A third form of faith developed later, as philosophy and science—belief in the power of the human mind. But philosophy and science are not the *common* good of all mankind; they are the possessions only of certain peoples and persons, in particular places, and at particular times.

Everything in the soul, as well as in life, appears first as a general activity before it particularizes itself in individuals. Originally, the song did not express personal emotions, but tribal sentiments; originally, it is an entire people which sings. So, originally, it was the common, national imagination that was creative. The poetry of individuals developed only after there was a common, national poetry.

In the beginning it is the people who create the language, the customs, the religious outlooks, the conceptions and ideas of things, for individuality is still weak and dependent.

Architecture, the first of all the arts, expresses the common mood of an entire people or an entire epoch. Its monumental works are not for individuals but for the community, for the city. All the great and mighty creations of history, common to all peoples and all times—religious and political—are the products of that architectural spirit which is common to all men and all times, and even to nature, which builds the common and the great first, and then proceeds to the ever more individualized forms of vegetation, animals and man.

In prehistoric times and in antiquity, the individual was entirely subjugated to the community, which determined his entire development and personality in way of life, in emotion and in thought. The individual was submerged in the tribe and state, and the undeveloped individuality brought about primitive collectiveness in everything. At first there was neither individual marriage, nor private property.

CHAPTER XI

Since the particular and individual develop from an earlier unity, all individual things are parts of previously existing wholes. The whole is prior to the parts, the one precedes the many.

At first the cosmos was a great, chaotic, individual whole. Later, there developed in it mechanical, physical and chemical forces, and the celestial bodies. In the same way, in the beginning, man and nature presented a whole, a unity, from which afterwards man separates through the development of his mind, and forms another entity.

Similarly, primitive mankind was the whole from which the individual parts and elements—the races, tribes and peoples—developed only later. All of mankind passed through that primordial phase—the phase of natural life, of savagery. But in the later, higher stages only certain parts of mankind participate.

There was a time when religion and philosophy, science and poetry, formed a chaotic whole in the myth, from which the individual parts developed only later.

There was a time when written pictures expressed a whole thought, as the child at first understands an entire phrase without attributing meanings to its individual words; later pictures stood for words, then for syllables; and only after these steps did they stand for single sounds. Originally, only entire passages could be printed. Gutenberg merely harvested a ripe thought when he cut the letters into separate units, so that they could be combined and separated, instead of preparing an entire passage on one plate.

The type is a whole from which exemplars separate later. Likewise, species and genera are the wholes from which particular individuals develop.

Accordingly, the type precedes the exemplar; the genus, the species precede the individual.

In nature genera always appear in a prototype of the whole class; general types are the first to appear, and only later particular, individual representatives. The lower, the more primitive the form, the more unlimited and exclusive is the predominance of type, and the weaker the individual characteristics. In the plant world there are no individuals; there are only genera. The individual plant is not differentiated from its fellows, while in the animal world the individual is slightly more differentiated from the others in its species. Yet it is only in the world of man, in the world of personality, that every individual is its own species, both mentally and physically. The animal does not have an individual will; whatever it does is done under the pressure of its genus and the past; whatever it does is done of necessity. One of the bases of human progress is the appearance of the unique, free "should" in the mature man.

Mankind existed for a long time as a species before races, tribes, and peoples developed. And originally the individual man was sunk into race, tribe, people and state; he lived the life of the genus. For once the influence of the family and state was unlimited and individual freedom was unrecognized. Progress was required for the individual gradually to free himself from the pressure of the group; so that he might be responsible for his own actions and so that responsibility for individual action fell no longer on the group, the tribe. Likewise, the ancient tribal aristocracy was superseded by the wealthy, individualistic aristocracy.

Man's first creations are the type for all succeeding ones. Later discoveries and inventions are based on the first; without fire, language, and agriculture there would be no later ones.

Architecture, the first of the arts, has nothing to do with the individual. Not only does it typify the life of a whole people, or a whole epoch, it is the prototype of all the later arts, as astronomy serves as prototype for all the later sciences. The real significance of Darwin's theory lies in his endeavor to transpose to organic nature the mechanical concept which Newton applied to the cosmos, to consider organic life in terms of cosmic laws. Thus, Newton's discovery of gravitation altered human ideas in all other regions of speculation, and all the rest of human thinking developed from the ideas of astronomy. To reduce all the laws in all fields of human thought to [the exactness of] the laws of astronomy would be to reach the ideal stage of reason.

CHAPTER XII

*Individual parts, forms, and elements separate
from a primal and undivided whole, and this separation of the particular from the general is the
basic condition of all higher life, of all the progress of consciousness and reason.*

Man has been able to separate himself progressively
from the rest of the world only through observation,
by seeing external reality ever more clearly as separate and distinct from himself. In this process he acquired, by degrees, his distinct internal life; becoming
more independent in movement and more and more
free from that general external pressure and stimulation which always directs the life of plants and animals, man has progressively created a free, internal
world, the world of the humane. On this contrast between man and nature rests the whole progress of
mind and civilization.

The history of man, in the dark, early times of his
existence, was not yet separated from the soil. Only
later, with slowly awakening consciousness, by coming
into the light, man slowly separated and freed his life
from the general life of nature. More and more he is
separating the *must* from the *should,* on which everything humane is founded.

In its failure to distinguish soul from body, the
primitive mind fails to separate the fantastic, the po-
tential, and the ideal from the real; it does not dif-

ferentiate sense perceptions from the activity of the reason, the world of spirit from the sensible world of reality, the internal from the external. The separation of the relative from the absolute constitutes the main difference between modern and ancient philosophies. In the latter, the absolute and the relative were unseparated. Thus, it was from the idea of motion, as a whole, that there separated, as parts, the ideas of space and time. In the first decades of the last century physicists failed to distinguish motion from matter; they considered all individual forms of motion (such as heat and light) as consisting of immeasurably small particles of matter. Just as originally man was not aware of the spectral structure of light, so air and water used to be thought of as elements, as entities; it was only later that chemistry isolated the individual elements of which they are composed. Similarly, until the microscope was invented, it was believed that human and animal bodies are homogeneous.

Religion could develop only after man had broken away from nature, after he had perceived the world in relation to himself. At first, religion was a whole, a type of the spirit, from which the great individualities of the historical mind of man—the arts, philosophies and sciences—appeared only later. The mythical stage of the human spirit is that primordial stage in which the particular, individual forms of historical life have not yet separated from the religious, chaotic, unorganized whole. In that liquid state of the human spirit everything floats in religion in an embryonic form.

Originally, every activity and every thing in life carried within itself the character of holiness. Fire was first produced artificially by the priests to be used in tribal rituals. Agriculture was then a religious activity, and, at that time, the reproductive process was considered to be a divine function. And because religion embraced at first all activities, the priests, as mediators between the gods and the people, were the first aristocrats, the first rulers and judges, the first teachers of the people. Here, it is the priest who is the primitive whole from which later separate king and judge, teacher and philosopher.

Throughout all antiquity peoples and states were religious communities; religion used to be national and official. Since the state and the people were not separated from religion, nor the lay authority from the ecclesiastic, the antagonism between them could not appear and there was no conflict between state and religion. The entire progress of the modern era starts with the separation of state from religion, because, when the church lost its secular power, it could no longer keep science in its service and prevent free inquiry.

In the same way, ethical duty separated from the external religious activities of the cult, and moral consciousness from religious consciousness. Fate and divine will were the first principles of human activity; only later could *morality* be divorced from religion. Instead of human destiny being determined by outside influences, by the gods, man, with increasing maturity, carries more and more of it in himself. In the same way *law* was a part of religion; the customs sanctioned by religion embraced all law as all morality. Even later, when human societies matured to the level of legality, the ancient peoples received their first laws from the gods (Moses). For this reason the clergy was the sole judge, the only interpreter of the law, in the early lives of both ancient and modern peoples.

71

Similarly, *the arts* were subject to, and a part of religion. Among all peoples religion gave birth to the higher forms of *architecture,* which began among all of them as the servant of religion. Religious themes were the subjects of all early sculpture and painting. The first portraits in wood, stone, and paint were of deities. *Poetry,* likewise, was unseparated from cult and religion; the early epic was concerned with the struggle of gods and demons; the first poem was the hymn, the first lyrics were poured out in praise of the gods. At first drama was also incorporated in religion; it formed part of the religious service, and among all peoples it originated in the religious celebrations and performances of the cults of particular deities.

The original problems of *philosophy* are the problems of religion; religion is the foundation of every philosophy. Just as the teaching of Thales arose from Greek theology, so all the ancient and classical philosophies were developed by the critics of religious interpretations, who doubted the truthfulness of religious ideas. Even in modern times questions of religion were the first problems of philosophy. Just as the origin of dualism in philosophy is found in the conflict between good and evil deities, just as the idea of metempsychosis is the original form of the concept of transmutation, so religious faith in destiny is the basic notion behind the idea of permanent and unchanging laws, and religious prophecies and oracles are the first manifestation of a deep longing of the human spirit—the longing to forecast, which is the final goal of all philosophy and science.

Science itself was originally in the service of religion, as an instrumental part; priests everywhere were the first teachers and possessors of all sorts of knowledge. *Astronomy* was first elaborated by the priests; it was the

Chaldeans who separated it from astrology, and made it a science, independent of religion. Among all the ancient peoples *medicine* was in temples, in the hands of priests. The *history* of nations was at first only a part of the history of their gods, and was written by priests.

As the temples were the first dwellings of the gods, the first hospitals, the first schools, the first observatories, libraries and theaters, and as the priests were the first guardians and cultivators of all the humanities—so the altars, temples, churches and monasteries, where the people gathered, were the first common holy places, binding together scattered parts of tribes and peoples.

In ancient times the sciences and humanities were not yet separated from poetry; originally sage and poet were one and the same, for poetry was undivorced from morality, philosophy and religion. In that age philosophy was an undivided whole embracing all the sciences. It was only later that mathematics separated, with astronomy, mechanics and physics, from philosophy. Mechanics and physics then separated from mathematics and astronomy, and from physics at last developed chemistry and meteorology. Psychology was the last to separate from philosophy; until recently the psyche was one of the main objects of metaphysical research. Law separated from morality only with Grotius; still later history separated from geography, and from moral and practical instruction.

So, originally, mankind was a whole from which the distinct and individual parts developed only gradually. It first existed as an entity—as genus and species; a long time passed before the great individualities of races, tribes and peoples separated from it.

In the first phases of the state, military and political power, along with property, were an undivided whole, the possessions of the class of warriors. Modern personal liberty and political rights rest on the separation of right from property, and of property from power. Just as the first water clocks contained measures for weight as well as time, so the functions of the individual parts and classes of society were not at first separated from the original community of labor, where everyone used to do all the work necessary to satisfy his own needs.

Just as the early family was undifferentiated, so the social relationships in tribal societies were not distinct from the political, private relationships and rights from the public. In the first states society was not yet separated from the political state, and the political state and the society were not yet separated from the people.

CHAPTER XIII

Since the ever smaller things separate from the great, primordial, general unity, it follows that the great precedes the small.

Organic life began in those regions of the earth where natural forces are great and where there is a surplus of that energy from which the organic world lives; man, likewise, first appeared in such regions, and, living the life of nature, he could not, in those climes, lift himself above a more or less passive existence, which was based on his feeling of weakness in comparison to the tremendous forces of nature. Later, men moved to those regions of the earth where natural forces are less exuberant, and where nature itself is easier to subdue. Here he became more active. The energy of nature in these regions being less, he was not given so many of life's necessities, but was left much more to himself and his own resources.

The first steps of man along the pathway from natural life toward civilization and humanity were the greatest of all that he made. Language, fire, agriculture, family, writing: These were the first mountains of humanity to rise above the ocean of animal life, the first and longest threads which man followed out of the darkness of nature and from which he spun his entire civilization; they are those titanic elements which began the creation of the history of mankind;

by means of them man gained mastery over nature, and was able to expand the realm of civilization over the whole surface of the earth. All later discoveries and inventions are merely developments of these first great ones.

The process of the creation of the world began with the action—in the inorganic realm—of the great forces of gravitation, heat, fire and water, and it was only when the struggle of these great inorganic forces died away that the action of the feebler organic forces, reproduction, heredity and adaptation, commenced. Just as the smaller astral bodies, such as planets and moons, separated from the great ones, the suns, so man first noticed regularity and natural law in the movement of the great, celestial bodies, then in those of lesser, earthly affairs. Astronomy, the science of the astral bodies, is the first science, for the awakened human mind first put and solved the greatest questions, those concerning the creation of the world, the nature of God, the first cause and final purpose of everything. It was only later that the regularity and natural law which man noticed among larger bodies of the sky came to be looked for in little things by man—in the phenomena of nature and of human society.

Thus, the birth and development of the world was explained first in terms of the great elements and forces: water, fire and air. The concept of minute atoms from whose combinations everything develops came only later. Similarly, the telescope was invented before the microscope, and it was first used for magnifying, then for measuring. So the basic laws in every science, as "the law of great numbers" in statistics, first draw the broad lines, the outlines. The regularity and conformity to law in the lesser phenomena of human life, in space and time, can be found and recognized only if one takes into consideration great intervals of space and time and great numbers.

As sense perception is the first experience of man, as man first notices the great, the first and strongest impressions are caused by the visible and sensible greatness. Thus, in early human history only the great phenomena were observed; at first history was preoccupied solely with the great and important events and personalities, which rose above the surface of the ordinary. The historical process was regarded as the result of activity of great personalities; events were considered the products of their wills; inventions, discoveries and ideas were ascribed to the intellectual powers of great individuals. Probing more and more deeply into the life of mankind, history increasingly turns from the great, brilliant and powerful toward the little, the unremarkable, the obscure; in place of the savage worship of greatness there develops more and more a mature and humane appreciation of labor; civilization is increasingly becoming a glorification of labor. Work is becoming the first article of religion and of civilization. It is ever more clearly realized that the entire progress of mankind is the result of the toil of those millions of common, unknown people who live and die in darkness, unrecorded by history, that the whole complex of present civilization is spun from the tiny, fragile threads of the work and lives of millions of little individuals.

Thus, there is a parallel between the development from the idea that fire, water and air are the first elements from which all phenomena arose, to the notion of the atom; and the succession from the idea that the history of mankind is the result of the activity of great personalities, their wills and their minds, to

77

the idea of history as the result of the feeling, the thinking, the endeavors, and the labor of the little, common people, who are indeed the atoms of civilization.

Originally, imagination also was occupied with the large; the first art, architecture, is the art of size; it first created colossal, cyclopic buildings; the colossal is the first phase of the idea of the beautiful. Only sculpture, a later art, began to descend toward smaller and smaller dimensions. The first epic sings of gods and titans, just as the first, empty pages of man's history were written out with the names of heroes and demigods.

CHAPTER XIV

*Since man's separation from nature began the
separation of the internal world from the external, man naturally observes first the outer world,
and only then himself.*

As a primitive, man, like the child, first becomes
aware of the external world; the observation of outer
reality is the first activity of the awakened mind. Only
at a higher and later stage of spiritual development,
among mature and civilized peoples, the observation
passes from nature, from the external world to the
internal, to the life of man. The science of man could
develop only after the natural sciences had reached a
high level; the history of mankind, as the broadest
science of man, will become a true science only after
the natural sciences prepare the ground and the
material for it.

Likewise, in the beginning of history the struggle of
man for the necessities of life was directed entirely
outward; it was a struggle against seas and rivers, land
and water, beast and jungle, cold and darkness. Later,
much later, that struggle was transferred to man, and
became more and more inward. Thus far man and
man's progress and civilization have been refreshed
and fortified from the outside, by the infusion of
fresh ethnical elements, by the entrance of new
peoples, who continued the work and the progress of
the exhausted groups. So far the movements within

mankind have arisen as a result of exterior forces. But there is ever less possibility of such external revitalization; new peoples are not so likely to intervene and lay the bases of new civilizations. Mankind is beginning to revive and refresh itself from the inside, from within itself. Men's minds are no longer being stimulated so much by particular events (such as the discovery of America); their acts are beginning to arise more and more from their own strength; more and more the stimulus for action is found in the depth of life, in history.

As man is moved first by external stimuli—physical forces, physical needs and blind impulses—and only later by ideas arising from the internal depths, from historical life, so the primary stimuli of every civilization are purely external and natural, such as the situation and fertility of the soil, and the climate. It is only later, as the depth of history grows, that the internal, deeper stimuli of civilization make themselves felt.

At first, religion is only a cult of external forces and of the phenomena of nature, and ritual, the external part of religion, is the principal element. Only with the increasing maturity of the religious spirit and with Christianity do external religious customs lose more and more their importance, with religion becoming an internal affair, a matter of the spirit.

The first moralities are also external. Just as in the beginning, man is moved and carried by external nature and its physical forces, so he first ties his happiness and destiny to external forces and things. The motives of his actions come from the outside—profit, vanity and fear of gods and of people. Then, as a result of hard effort, pain and struggle, conscience appears and becomes stronger as the soul becomes cultivated, ultimately determining the entire life of conscious, mature man.

The first phase of every science is the description and classification of things according to their external characteristics. At first the subject of history was only the external sense life of peoples; it consisted of descriptions of external life and visible deeds.

Likewise, the higher life of civilization always begins on the edges of continents; only later does it penetrate into their depths.

CHAPTER XV

Every individual part, which has separated
from the whole of life, wills to live according to its
particular individuality, to be a whole in itself. It
must, therefore, struggle continually not only
against the whole from which it has divorced, but
also against all the other separated parts.

Thus, with the separation of the particular
from the general comes struggle, destruction,
pain. The first phase of every free action is de-
struction, and the first characteristics of free and
individual life are hostility and waste.

The original relationships between man and man,
their first encounters, were hostile and strife-ridden.
The art of murder was the first and most important
skill of man, arms were his first tools, plunder was his
first economy. At all times and places it is arms which
clear the way for commerce and civilization. The
peoples of Europe destroyed the ancient civilizations
before they erected, on their ruins, their own, new
ones. Likewise, the first impact of the European civilization on all the natural, barbaric cultures is fatally
disruptive.

The State, in order to unify, had to wage a deadly
struggle against the tribes. Destroying, at its beginning, the ancient gods and ideas, Christianity destroyed the very foundations of ancient civilization,

and only on the rubble did it begin to build the temple of the one God, in which all peoples will find shelter. The case of science is similar: In order to free itself, it had to carry on, at first, a bitter struggle with religion and metaphysics.

Similarly, destruction is the first phase of nature's influence on man. Fire was originally known by its destructive qualities; electricity made its appearance in the hostile thunderbolt.

The first gods were enemies of the people; they aroused only the emotions of fear, envy and wrath, but never of love; the cult of evil spirits was the first phase of religion.

Thus, everything new in history first brings evil; all reforms, inventions, discoveries, all new ideas, turn on the old to destroy it. Pain awakens life; doubt awakens consciousness; the first song is the wail of anguish and grief. Tragedy develops before the comedy: the tragic talent precedes the comic.

CHAPTER XVI

The conflict between these numerous forces, forms and independent wholes results in a diminution in their number; the struggle for predominance forces a reduction in the number of the contestants.

As the unity of consciousness develops only in slow, successive stages as the last and highest result of many sense impressions, the atoms of the spirit, so out of many impressions, only a few rise to the level of perception and of many perceptions only one becomes the image of the object. Likewise, from many thoughts and ideas only one becomes the theory, the principle, the formula for millions of facts, just as the great social ideas become formulae for millions of people, the organization of their aspirations and strivings.

In language also the thousands of primordial vocables are reduced to the few which gained supremacy over all the others. At first, every tribe and district, every city had its dialect, but these many were in time reduced to one national language. Once every written word had its own picture, but that originally enormous multitude was reduced in time to twenty or thirty characters, which are to language what the few tens of elements, to which all the materials and phenomena can be reduced, are to chemistry.

The numerous spirits, the many deities of the ancients were, with time, also reduced in number. From the worship of many forces man began to render particular homage to One. Once every family and every tribe had its own particular deities; some of these arose to the dignity of national deities, and Christianity lifted one of them to the position of God for all men.

In science each group of facts was explained by a separate principle; special fluids were believed the causes of heat, light, and electricity.

For early man each phenomenon, each object, is an entity, a separate type, a whole. Likewise, the early historian believes every outstanding personality to be a whole, a type in its own right, while with progress the explanation of historical phenomena tends to be reduced to a few higher laws. In every science the number of principles and laws is being progressively reduced, just as in religion the mind progresses from belief in many gods toward belief in One, from whom all things originate, and to whom all things return.

In the same way the many initially independent families become reduced to tribes, and the many tribes to a few peoples. Also, mankind develops at first in many convenient localities, in many separate, independent centers, and each of these peoples has, at first, its own particular consciousness; each of them for itself is mankind. Thus, the age of many independent tribes is the age of feudalism of mankind. Similarly, polytheism, an age of many independent gods, may be called religious feudalism, in the same sense in which feudalism may be called social polytheism. Likewise, the many individual sciences are to one intellect what the many peoples are to one mankind.

CHAPTER XVII

Thus, the process of reduction is, from another viewpoint, the process of concentration.

The original, or natural, civilizations were scattered on a natural basis, at all the points where nature was favorable to their development. At last, they began developing in only one direction, and, by the process of diffusion from these original points, the civilization of mankind is becoming more and more one single unity.

In the first societies creativity was equally distributed among the entire population; the whole people created customs, poetry, art and religion; the whole people thought; only later this ability became concentrated in a few individual spirits.

The process of concentration leads from the *changing* toward the fixed and *permanent*. Man began to settle permanently in definite localities only with the development of agriculture and of cults regarding "holy places." Wandering, nomadism, constitute the first stages of social life. Civilization today is still in the nomadic stage; thus far it has changed its earthly habitats many times. Every civilization was developed by a new, fresh human group; yet one day the civilization of man will stabilize itself and find its fixed and permanent centers. We see also in the history of peoples the primitive rule of individual and changing wills being ever more reduced to governments of fixed and unchanging laws which regulate all human affairs. Likewise, the primitive measures of space and time were various, unreliable and changing. In modern scientific research there is much less confusion than there used to be. Similarly, today's ships travel surely and directly, by means of the compass, quite free from their former uncertainties.

Thus, with the increasing progress of the intellect and with a more accurate knowledge of the laws of history, the future of the human species will also become increasingly clearer, and the final end of the entire historical process will be increasingly better understood. Progressing along a visible and sure path, there will be less and less of the hesitations and wanderings to which so far peoples have been exposed. There will result fewer fruitless struggles, and less squandering of energy in darkness. By uniting all its forces in one direction, mankind will go faster and more surely toward the final goal of the historical process.

And as man's destiny depended originally on external accidents and possibilities, so the early religions proclaimed the rule of whimsical deities. At that remote time man linked his fate to the unreliable will of particular gods, to tiny external incidents (such as the entrails of sacrificial animals, or the flight of birds). Until they came to the permanent and rational rule of One God, men and peoples could not have a clear and definite way before them.

Man first notices the unusual, the extraordinary. Air was first observed as wind, electricity as lightning bolt. Only later, with progress and maturity, the intellect began to study the ordinary phenomena of the life of man and of nature, and endeavor to explain the unusual, extraordinary and irregular by means of the common, ordinary and unvarying.

In the first stages of his development, man lives, like the child, only the life of the emotions. His mind is a liquid mass without a solid kernel, without a central self in which coagulates the entire life of the psyche. Similarly, the enormous liquid masses of the life and history of entire peoples, their philosophical systems and their great literatures finally condense into a few thoughts and ideas, at a few fixed and elevated points. Just as a proverb is the condensation of an entire story, a description of an entire event or adventure, the few letters in modern writing are the concentration of the enormous original mass of hieroglyphic pictures.

In the process of condensation and solidification, phenomena become concentrated, smaller. Accordingly, (see Ch. XIII) *the great precedes the small*. With increasing density phenomena acquire an ever greater depth. *This is the process from the extensive toward the intensive*. In the beginning of its historical existence every people is expansive; it tries to extend itself as much as possible, by the conquest and subjugation of other countries and peoples. Only later there develops a period of intensity in its life. So every new doctrine, theory and idea, on its first appearance, begins to act aggressively; it expands in all directions, and embraces even those fields from which, later, it will have to retreat.

CHAPTER XVIII

The influence of certain forces expands in all directions only from individual, fixed and elevated points. The process of concentration develops a new process of generalization, the process of expansion from the narrowness of the particular to the broadness of the universal.

Heat and light in the solar system could begin to expand in all directions from a single point, the sun, only after its planets had lost their own heat and luminosity and when heat and light remained concentrated on the sun alone. The life of the earth and of all things upon her results from her single relationship to the sun.

Every idea which is accepted by the many and which is a part of the common heritage was first conceived in the consciousness of an individual. Later it expanded over the masses of society and over time. All the social ends and plans and all the great ideas which move the masses were once the ends, plans and ideas of individuals. Every public and common thought is originally the thought of a single person. All civilization and all development of the human spirit originate in the elevated individual personality, in whom is concentrated the force and who expresses the striving of an entire people or era. Every great idea first erupts from an individual mind, and from this historical height the light of its discoveries expands through ever wider circles. As the light of the sun first shines upon the pinnacles of mountains, and then descends into the depth of plains, so every new light in history first illuminates the heads of elevated, noble personalities, and then descends into the social valleys. And just as the sunlight does not illuminate everything at once, but gradually descends to ever lower places, so the great truths do not achieve complete power over society at once; men of consciousness and reason first fight for them; then they spread to ever larger circles, embracing more and more people, just as the originally narrow human consciousness expands with progress, enveloping more and more things over ever increasing vistas of space and time.

Even in ancient Egypt there existed a theory of astronomy according to which only Venus and Mercury circle the sun; Copernicus extended this truth to all the planets, establishing the principle of heliocentrics. Similarly, Kepler noticed first that the orbit of Mars is not circular but elliptical, then he expanded this discovery to all the planets with his first law: The orbits of all the planets are elliptical. The force of gravitation which Newton discovered in earthly phenomena was later expanded by him to all the astral bodies; in this way he developed the principle of gravitation. After the laws of astronomy were established, the notion of law was extended from the cosmos to all earthly things: first to inorganic phenomena, then to organic; now the idea of natural law is being applied even to the minute and complicated phenomena of human society and mind, in their historical development. Thus the idea of organism expands in all directions; thus psychology, from the study of man's mind, extends to the study of the soul of peoples, societies and epochs.

History began with the recorded description of individual, local actions and events, the accounts of peoples and times in biographies and chronicles. Covering, in the course of its development, progressively greater spans of time, history is embracing more and more aspects and phenomena of human life in space and time—customs, laws, religion, art and language, philosophy and science, literature and technology, and all other forms of social existence as well; history's preoccupation is changing from the individual hero, the particular people, the specific era, to all mankind, at all times. So history expands progressively from man and his life in all directions and to all things; it can be realized more clearly now that not only man and his mind have a history, but everything else on earth, and the earth as well, and the cosmos.

The idea of right outgrows the narrow limits of privilege, extending through ever larger circles. Freedom, justice, education, civilization, all the great acquired goods of man, are still in the process of spreading from special classes, tribes, peoples and times to become the common right of ever greater parts of mankind.

As man's geographical knowledge developed from familiarity with local points and regions to comprehension of the entire earth, so the other sciences expanded in all directions from only a few points. In the process the names of particular areas were extended to entire lands and continents. (Africa was once the name applied only to the northeastern part of that continent.)

It was only after the original multitude of ideographs had been reduced to a few letters that the value and meaning of each character expanded to a general application and meaning in all words. In the same manner, words at first expressed only one characteristic of a thing, later this characteristic was extended to indicate the whole object.

Thus, with increasing progress, the field of human feelings and sympathies, at first restricted to a few things and persons, extends to larger and larger numbers. National character is, at the beginning, simply the character of one tribe, which spreads its rule over the others. National religions, customs and laws originate in this way. Political and social rights, limited at first to the conquering group, expand, in the process of history, through larger and larger circles. For all social struggles, and all new forms of social and political life, always originate at definite points, in definite regions, and thence become disseminated to ever more distant areas.

The great development of man's economy, the progress of his spiritual and material culture, was made possible by the fact that he extended the working ability of his hands by means of tools and machines. And with the elevation of the economic standards of society the possibility of a better and more humane life for the masses increases.

Commerce, industry, and the trades all developed first in particular localities; it was the discovery of America that brought about worldwide commerce and industry. So today industry produces not only for the particular classes, but for the ever broader masses of society. Commerce and industry are continually being extended to more and more peoples and regions.

In all past times education was limited only to certain aspects of man's mind; modern education tries to cultivate the entire man, to educate him in all his aspects, to develop all his potentialities. Formerly, education was restricted to the upper classes of society and the right to education was the privilege of the elite in all societies.

We notice that the mind of man, expanding more and more in the fields of reason, augments the area of human morality, and that the larger the field of understanding becomes, the larger is the range of human sympathy. Civilization began in isolated but convenient parts of the earth—one might say, in its aristocratic locales. With the increasingly successful struggle against nature, man extended his civilization from these potent but separated centers to cover the whole earth.

Wealth, education, power, higher religion, and more enlightened thoughts and customs were first the possession of a few—individuals, families, tribes or peoples, classes or cities; from these they expanded to increasingly larger masses, as the cult of individual deities grew into the idea of one common God, as particular laws of science are reduced to fewer and fewer general principles, as particular tribes become peoples, and particular peoples the archetype of one mankind.

CHAPTER XIX

Since the expansion from the particular to the general occurs from fixed and elevated points, the succession of events in nature and in society is from above downwards. The process of expansion implies the process of descending.

As all life on earth, and the earth herself, originated from the sun, so the solid ground which was the basis of all higher organic forms, including man, originally consisted of the mountain peaks which were the first to rise above the waters.

And as the sun first illumes the mountain peaks, before its light descends into the valleys and plains, the light of consciousness first illumes the highest peaks of the mind—every new idea first lights the heights of reason and consciousness—then it penetrates down to the depths of life and society. All the great social ideas originate in particular elevated minds; it is there that all great thoughts mature. Every new truth is first accepted by people of *reason* and *consciousness;* and much later by the emotional masses of society.

The overwhelming primary impressions come from the sky; the motions of sun and stars are the first familiar and regular events apparent to the eye. Man first noticed regularity in astronomical phenomena and astronomical regularity impressed itself as a type on all the other regions of man's mind. The notion of law, of order, was taken from the sky and applied to the earth and to men; the principle of motion was carried down from astronomy to other sciences.

Philosophy was concerned in the beginning with the loftiest problems, the beginning of the world, the first cause, and so on. Only later did it descend from metaphysical heights to more fruitful plains, from sky to earth.

Man's history started in the sky, in those early days when the gods who dwelt there interfered in human affairs, and when the stars determined his destiny. And when history became earthbound it first recorded the highest strata of society, the glittering crust of kings and aristocrats. Only in modern times has history descended deeper into society, embracing successively more of the complete life of peoples and of mankind.

And as all of man's history began in the skies, so did all his advances and benefits descend from above— language, literacy, fire, agriculture and tools—all these were originally given to men by the gods. Only much later was it recognized that all these goods are man's own acquisitions, the results of long efforts, struggles and experiences. Man himself has in his mental progress descended from God's creature, a being little lower than the angels, to the status of the last and most perfected of the animals. Similarly, all activities—reproduction, fire making, agricultural processes, and so on—were at first sacred activities, which only with time descended from the holy place to the commonplace.

It was only with the appearance of Buddha and Jesus, who preached to the lowly and needy, the masses, that religion became social and democratic. The first religions were purely natural and aristocratic;

with Christianity the truths of religion and the sacred books began to penetrate the masses of society.

Among all peoples dwellings were first erected for the gods; *then* for men; sculpture, starting with the elaboration of the head, descended from divine types to portraits of the common man. Gods were the original heroes of drama; only with Euripides are the heroes brought down from the height of divinity to the plain of humanity; the destiny of his heroes is no longer determined from above, by the gods; Euripedes put their fate in the depths of their own souls.

The light of history began to illuminate the peaks of human society while the valleys were still shrouded in the darkness of prehistoric life. Only later in the historical process all man's great acquisitions—freedom, education, political and social rights, law and morality—descended from the heights of society and became increasingly the common good of the masses. Once virtue was the privilege of the upper classes; the lower orders had only obligations.

Laws first came from above, from the gods, and originally they were at once codes of civil society and rules of moral life.

As man descends more and more from the heights of divine origin to the animal; as from the heights of temple and palace the light of consciousness and justice descends to the ever lower strata of society; as economics based on gold and silver descends to economics of iron and steel; as man's interest in sky and nature is lowered to himself; as from the heights of the sterile principle of authority the mind descends to the fertile valleys of experience—so, gradually, from the mountain heights men descended to the plains and lowlands.

Privilege is the first form of every right, just as *luxury is the first form of every necessity*. All the great goods of man descend from the restricted level of luxury and expand to the status of common needs. Commerce begins with the importation from abroad of luxury articles for the upper classes; in time it begins to deal in ordinary commodities. Industry makes the luxury of clothing a necessity. Printing changes education and culture from an indulgence of the wealthy into the necessity of the vastly more numerous poor. All man's goods and acquisitions, all the products of his labor, descend from the excessively *expensive* to the *cheap* and ordinary.

CHAPTER XX

The individual wholes which have separated from the primordial general unity tend, after a time, to unite, so that, instead of being independent wholes, they become more and more dependent parts of a single great unity. This process is a succession from dispersion toward concentration and unity, from discontinuity toward continuity.

The earth, in passing from a molten, luminous condition lost her independence as an entity, and became only a part of the great whole of the solar system, dependent upon the sun. Likewise, in human society each family and each tribe is at first an independent community living its separate life. Every people, likewise, at its beginning, lives a separate existence, and constitutes an independent whole. Only among modern peoples, connected by identical material and spiritual ties, is the idea of common interests awakened to ally them more and more into one great whole. This unification of peoples into an ever greater mankind is mainly the result of the fundamental interest of man—his living conditions and economy. As the first higher societies were the result of the application of human labor to the soil, so the progress of culture, by binding the particular peoples to their lands, directs them more and more strongly towards one another; each people is becoming increasingly necessary to all other peoples; every group becomes more and more only a part of a larger unity. Each people, each country, as it progresses, needs all the others for its food and maintenance. These well-understood common interests make for stronger and more permanent unity among peoples and men than any other forces.

The civilization of each people formed, at the beginning, an isolated and independent whole unrelated to others. But the civilization of mankind is becoming more and more one; the history of man is traveling ever more in only one direction, and toward one goal. Since mankind is one, its history is one, for men live their history only once; therefore, all the great inventions and discoveries, all great ideas and theories, appear only once. And that the civilizations of individual peoples are not independent wholes in themselves is obvious from the fact that the threads of history are ever more interlaced, so that the history and civilization of one people cannot be understood without a knowledge of the history of other peoples, contemporary as well as ancient. Civilizations of all modern peoples are rooted in classical antiquity; all of their spiritual life is only the result of a long previous process of history. The first elements of the history of this one mankind developed organically and naturally only once; only once were laid the foundations for its entire civilization. All later civilizations are only additions to this one building. Similarly, the particular classes and strata of society, which formerly were sharply separated according to ethnic origin, wealth, rights and education, are becoming increasingly connected with one another by strong, organic ties.

Now that astronomy has bound the earth to the

cosmos, and biology the animals to the earth, and man to the animals, and psychology the soul of man to the soul of the animal, it remains for scientific history to bind man to man. The understanding of history increasingly binds natural man to the historical, and civilization is ever more strongly bound to the obscure beginnings of man's life on the earth. History must demonstrate the fact that in the shadows of the primitive life of mankind, in its first struggles with nature, the basis for all progress was laid. All the greatest and most difficult achievements were gained then; then it was that the fundamental discoveries and inventions occurred which were indispensable to all later progress, and from which all later inventions and discoveries are merely the derivations and consequences. Then it was that the organization of man's body, the permanent and unchanging *bearer* of his mind, was perfected. In those far-off times the whole course of mankind through history was laid out. All civilizations are only the flower and fruit of the tree whose roots lie deep in the darkness of the natural, animal life of man.

The great historical ideas—monotheism, gravitation, evolution—are not the results of the sense or of the present, but of the whole history of mankind; great spirits are not instruments of their times and their peoples, nor an expression of the present; they are the instruments of universal history, individual moments on the time-wound clock which is history. Hence, the development of great spirits can by no means be understood from the narrow environment in which they occurred, from the life of their society; they are the tools of all history, dependent only upon it and bound only to it. As the earth is the common mother of all human beings, so is history the common mother of all spirits; only history can give birth to spirits. The Jews did not produce Christ, nor did the English bring forth Newton and Darwin; when their time came, they were born by history, they belong only to history, they surpass their peoples and their times.

All that which is individual in history—be it peoples, religions, philosophies, sciences or civilizations—bound with ties of interdependence and continuity, is losing its independence and becoming part of that great whole which is the history of mankind. Thus all the artificial barriers with which egoism and unconsciousness have separated countries, peoples, religions and epochs are being destroyed. And while the process of the history of mankind develops in the individual peoples, the process of the history of the human mind is developing in the particular sciences.

Thus, history is to bind all peoples and all times; to bring them closer to one another and to reconcile them. By binding himself to nature and to its things and phenomena, and by understanding the laws of its life, man through history approaches it closer and closer, and makes peace with it. By multiplying his ties with an ever larger number of things, he develops an increasing interst in them, they become increasingly valuable, close and necessary to him, and he feels more indebted to an ever larger number of them; the narrow circle of his sympathies expands, with his fuller and deeper ties, to an ever larger number of things.

Thus, the attractive power of history, like that of the sun, is constantly growing; it increasingly attracts to itself all the dismembered parts of mankind and of its intellect, so that, today, primitive man is closer to civilized man than contemporary peoples were once to one another.

CHAPTER XXI

In order that all individual things might be bound into a single, great organic whole, each thing must assume its rightful place among other things, each must come in its own time, and must, therefore, possess determined limits in space and time; it must have precise limits of value, size and strength, which it cannot exceed without damaging other parts and organs of the whole. The value of everything is proportional to the necessity for it, to its size, quantity, strength and duration. Thus, the organization of things leads to proportion; organization is progress from disproportion to proportion.

Everywhere, at the first levels of development, parts develop disproportionately. In the first stages of psychic life disproportion appears as a predominance of sensuality and fancy over reason. Only with maturity does reason succeed in taking its place by reducing fantasy and pleasure to their proper limits. Originally, fear and hatred prevail over sympathy and love because emotion rules thought.

In the early societies and in the first phases of all societies, the political head has a disproportionate influence over all the other elements of society; among all peoples, so far, power, wealth and education, and all the other human goods and acquisitions were distributed among the social strata in a disproportionate way, and were always a source of internal struggles. Every people, as it originated, endeavored to expand its domination over other poeples through conquest and subjugation, and to retain all power and sources of wealth for itself alone. It was long before the individual peoples were limited to their own proper boundaries, proportional to their size and strength.

In the early times, religion was the autocrat of the human mind; it withdrew to its proper sphere only later, making room for philosophy and science. And in their turn, philosophy and science also tried to expand their rule over all regions of life, mind and spirit, and to know the absolute. Chemistry was first occupied with the search for the "philosopher's stone," for the elixir of life, for absolutes unattainable. Psychology first occupied itself with principles, substances, with the first cause, and with the soul. It is only in recent times that the sciences began to enter their proper bounds, which are defined by the other sciences and by the limits of the knowable. Only after many vain attempts were the limitations of the human mind defined. Like a child stretching out its hand to grasp the moon, the mind of man, in his childhood, tried to grasp and solve problems outside the limits of its power; it wanted to understand everything.

Every theory and idea, according to the succession of its appearance in the history of sciences, endeavors to suppress other ideas and theories; in chemistry, after the overthrow of the phlogistic theory, oxygen rose to supremacy; in geology and biology evolution arose against the theory of catastrophe, creation and unchangeability. Not until Kant were the rights of the senses, along with those of reason, recognized.

Art in its first phases is also disproportionate; the

most ancient figures of the gods are colossal or monstrous.

Consequences of proportion: Only when each thing occupies its proper place in space and in time beside other things, only when every thing will have determined the proper limits of its size, duration, strength, and value, will come balance and peace, and the harmony of the whole. The proper proportioning of things leads to balance, peace and harmony; it also brings to being all that is *beautiful and good: truth, freedom and justice.*

The first result of the proportionalization of all things will be: *one and only one whole.* Only after every thing has taken its proper place in space and time, beside all other things, the life of the whole will start. In order for the whole to exist, all the parts must be present; in order that all be present, none must occupy the place of another, it must not extend over its limits. In order to make a whole there must be proportion; the whole is the result of proportion. It is only in the great whole of the history of human life that one can see the regularity, the obedience to natural law, of every part. And only in that great unity can lasting *peace* be achieved, since peace is nothing other than the regular, lawful, harmonious and proportional movement of all the individual parts of the whole.

Since every individual thing depends on other things and could not exist except in its relations to these, nothing can be understood without considering its relation to other things; incomprehensible means unrelated, alone. Each thing can be understood only from its relations to all other things; only as a part of a whole. And because man is related to all the things in the past and present, and since he is a whole only in history, it follows that the whole is only in the history of man, and that all individuality can be completely understood only from the history of man and of his mind, for only the whole is comprehensible. The smaller the whole, the less one finds of reason in it, and vice versa. It follows that the highest *reason* is to be found only in the whole history of man, and that only in the whole of history can there be complete *truth*. Accordingly, the entire truth does not rest in any particular theory, idea, or principle, since these are only individual parts of the whole truth, are truths only for their particular times; for other epochs they are errors. Geocentrics, polytheism, and the divine origin of man were truths for their times; today they are errors, as heliocentrics, evolution and the equality of men would have been errors for the primitive human mind.

Since only the whole is truth, since only the whole can be understood, all individual things are reasonable, true and meaningful only when and so far as they are wholes. As soon as they stop being wholes, and become parts, organs of larger wholes, they make sense only when seen in relation to those wholes. Thus it is only in the whole history of man that one can see the truth and meaning of all things.

Regarded from particular epochs—"presents"— things which do not exist at the time appear as errors. Geocentrics, slavery, castes and polytheism were all true in their times, but the fact that those things were true can be seen only from the whole history of man and his mind.

It follows that everything individual is true only in its place and in its time, only in the determined limits of space and time; accordingly, in order that a thing may be understood, that it may make sense, that it may be true, it must have limits. Thus, truth is the determination of the precise limits of things in space and time; the more precise the limits, the higher the truth. Thus, heliocentrics is a higher truth than geocentrics, for it bounds the earth more precisely, in its size and energy relationships to the sun and the cosmos. In a similar way, Darwin's theory of descent with modification through natural selection is a higher truth than the theory of creations, for it determines more precisely the relations of man and his value toward the other animals and natural objects. It follows that error is nothing but a lack of precise knowledge as to the limits of things. Error is to truth as the child is to the mature man, the savage community to the civilized, the tribe to the nation, the nation to mankind. The idea of man can be truth only in the whole of mankind; only in mankind can one be a Man.

All individual truths are true only in their place. It is false to say that the earth is the center of the universe, or that man is a divinely chosen creature. It is true to state that the earth occupies a place among the sun's other planets and man his proper place among the other animals and things. Geocentrics is true only for the senses, while it is an error for the intellect.

Since the highest truth is one, changeless and eternal, all that is passing is not a complete truth. Accordingly, the highest truth cannot be found in one man, or one people, one religion, philosophy or science, or concerned with individual times or particular places. The highest truth that the human mind can attain is only in the whole history of man.

Thus reason and truth are only in the whole, and the whole is the result of proportion; truth and reason can be found only where and when there is proportion; the more precise the proportion, the more of truth and reason there will be.

Every *good*, also, exists only in proportion. Everything is good in its place and time; as soon as it passes these limits, it becomes evil (despotism, slavery, cruelty and ignorance of primitive men). Christianity brought about the disintegration of ancient society, and is today one of the greatest goods. Evil is a good of a lower degree; just as error is truth of a lower degree; evil is a narrow good, a good for just one man, one class, one people, or time; for other men, classes and times, it is evil. Accordingly, the fact that everything is good in its place and time can be seen only in the perspective of all history, and the highest good can only be achieved in history's entirety. The virtues are the virtues only of their place and their time.

The *need* and *value* of everything in its place and time, in its determined limits of quantity, size and strength can only be observed in the whole of history; the reason for the existence of all that was and still is, can be understood only with reference to the whole. Today neither pyramids, temples, slavery, clergy, nor conquest have the same value they had in ancient times, in the first phases of the life of men in states, just as in antiquity the press, railway, electricity would not have had their modern value. The press became a necessity only a few centuries ago, but agriculture and commerce were necessary since the beginning of men's social life, writing from the first civilization to the last, fire and tools from the beginning of man's life on the earth until its conclusion. One can see the value of religion, philosophy and science, of instinct, sense and reason, of great geniuses, and of the masses, of family, tribe and nation, of ideas, theories, and of man himself, only from the perspective of history.

One can arrive at more precise concepts of justice only by realizing that everything is necessary in its time and place, for justice also is the result of proportion, and the more precisely values may be determined, the more exact is justice. Like truth, justice reduces things to their proper limits and values according to their size, strength, and duration, and the more precise the limits, the higher is the justice. Moreover, justice, like truth, is too great and too sublime a principle to be seen in just one present, at one specific time, or in one particular place; the highest degree of justice can be found only in the whole of history. By realizing that all things are necessary in the limits of their place and time, and that all of them have value within those limits, one renders justice to all of them; the historical sense contracts the sphere of condemnation, of ridicule, of stupidity and sorrow ever more, while it expands those of justice and right.

Since justice is the result of the proper proportion of things, *injustice is the result of disproportion.* In previous human societies there has been no real justice, since so far neither money nor bread, power nor property, education nor freedom, rights nor duties have been distributed proportionally. Instead, among a given people or social class at any given time, there have been accumulated on the one side power and property, freedom, education, rights, and on the other, duties, poverty, slavery and ignorance.

Because everything is necessary and valuable in the determined limits of space and time, everything is just and righteous in its place and time.

Freedom is also the result of proportion; with increasingly precise proportion things find more and more freedom to move within their limits of space and time. And, as one can see the limits of the freedom of everything only in history as a whole, it follows that only in the whole of mankind can one attain the highest degree of freedom.

All *progress* strives for as precise proportions as possible between things and between people. All natural objects occupy their proper places in space and time; in their realm just proportions are already achieved. Thus, there is no more progress in nature, but only among men, in human society, where the proper proportions of things are not achieved as yet. Progress is the determination of precise limits for all things; the progress of modern peoples rests on the limitation of the power of religion, of the state, and of classes, so that science and philosophy, freed from their bondage, can expand with greater élan over broader fields. Likewise, the progress of the human mind was made possible by the drawing of limits for mental power, whereby spheres unattainable to the intellect were abandoned.

Beauty also is the result of the proportion of things, and the thirst for beauty is, in fact, the striving for proportion. Where proportion or limits do not exist there is no beauty; in early oriental art there was no proportion and, therefore, no beauty; it was dominated by the limitless and immeasurable.

As it is only from the whole of history that one can see that everything is true and reasonable, good and beautiful, and righteous in its place and time, it is obvious that the really beautiful and good, the really reasonable and true, the really free, just and moral, can exist only in the whole, only in all humanity.

All the *differences* among things in nature and in

110

human society are simply the results of various proportions of the same elements.

Since the whole is the result of proportion, and since every part occupies its proper place in the whole, every new part which is brought to birth exists and develops *at the expense* of all the other parts. The previously existing parts must be constricted and diminished to form a place for the new part. Higher forces develop only at the expense of the lower ones; humanity and civilization develop only at the expense of the animal in man; much has to be hewn away so that he can live in society. Reason increases at the expense of instinct; in order that reason may develop the senses must become dull; man must lose much of his primitive animal warmth and freshness before he can think. Reason develops only at the cost of the passions and the lower forces of the soul. It follows that the highest reason can be attained in history alone, for it is only from historical heights that one can reasonably judge people and things; the closer one is to events and people the more susceptible they are to one's feelings and interests. Among all peoples, literature flourishes after splendid political epochs, after the lower, more primitive forces have been spent on wars and struggles for material welfare. The perfection and independence of mankind and of all human history grows only at the expense of independence of particular peoples and times. If something in that great single whole is to rise, something else has to be lowered; for something to be strengthened, another thing must be weakened; if something expands or increases, something else diminishes.

In order that national and political life might begin, tribal influences, which in the beginning were very powerful and occupied the whole soul of man, had to be reduced. Likewise, in order that all mankind may begin to live humanely, it is necessary that the large groups of peoples, which heretofore have embraced all the highest interests and sympathies of man, and for whose maintenance all the energy of man has been consumed, be constricted and diminished. Similarly, in the beginning of historical times, the sphere of law was enormous; it determined and regulated everything; with increasing freedom the sway of law is being progressively reduced.

With nicer proportioning of things in human society, *economy* becomes more and more efficient. With the progressively more precise distribution of things in space and time, each part receives only as much of the energy of the whole as is necessary for its maintenance and development; the introduction of order into things brings about the saving of space and time.

Proportionalization of things makes that which was a whole in itself only a part of a new and more general whole. All the peoples which existed in history as independent wholes are becoming increasingly the parts and organs of one mankind and all special epochs are being integrated into the whole history of man as episodes and incidents.

Proportionalization leads to harmony and *general reconciliation*. Individual interests agree more and more with those of society, and the expansion of those interests makes human life ever more stable and harmonious. For example, modern intellect is increasingly reconciling religion and science, determining for each limits of value, strength and size. Every real truth, every great idea reconciles within itself many errors; mankind, as the highest truth, reconciles within itself all the successive errors of history—

particular times, people and tribes. Only the understanding of all history can reconcile all those contrasts
which successively appeared in time—the controversies between thoughts and things, men and nature,
spirit and matter, freedom and destiny. The increasing understanding of history reconciles all the oppos-
ing ideas and doctrines which successively appeared
in particular sciences and in philosophy and which
struggled to predominate as truths over one another,
contesting each other's truthfulness. So the latest concept that both fire and water participated in the creation and formation of the earth reconciles the two
antagonistic theories of geology, the neptunian and
the plutonian; in biology the principles of heredity
and adaptation are increasingly reconciled, for it is
realized more and more that both of these factors
have their roles in the appearance and development
of organic life. Likewise in geology, the theories of
catastrophes and revolutions are being more and
more reconciled to the principle of evolution.

The process of reconciliation leads to the process of
contemporization. Every form and every force, as each
successively appears in time, struggles for predominance over the others. When they attain a state of
proportion and balance they live simultaneously, each
its own life. The process of contemporization is a
movement from the successive toward the simultaneous.

Mankind developed successively in individual
peoples, tribes, states, and civilizations in various regions of the earth, and as the process continued, the
notion of one single and simultaneous mankind
began to emerge. Likewise, the process of the human
mind in history proceeded, in the beginning, successively in all fields, which formerly dominated over
one another—religion, art, philosophy and the sci-

ences. Only when one single mankind matures completely will there be enough room for peaceful coexistence and development of all these aspects, all these directions and elements in human life. Then spirit and history will develop calmly and live quietly side by side.

As the arts once developed successively—architecture, sculpture, painting—and today they all develop simultaneously, so the successive phases of mankind's history become simultaneous elements of modern society. The primitive era of natural man settles into the mass of civilized communities. The light of civilization first illumed men successively, in particular regions of the earth, until it began to enlighten more and more of humanity, simultaneously.

The proportionalization and contemporization of phenomena, which brings everything into mutually dependent and simultaneous existence, lead to organic alliances, to the *organization* of everything into one great system. At the highest level of the history of mankind all the elements of man's life, natural as well as historical, will be distributed and bound into one organism in such a way that none will predominate at the expense of the others, and that the general life of the entire organism will manifest itself only through the common and harmonious activity of all of them. And only in that one great organic whole can one arrive at complete morality, freedom, justice and truth.

CHAPTER XXII

Only from the standpoint of the Whole can one observe that all things are parts and organs of a single Unity, that all of them have one and the same ultimate source, are going in the same direction, toward the same goal, and that this Whole has occurred only once, and, accordingly, lives only once.

The history of mankind is a great tree whose roots are deep in the darkness of prehistoric life; all religions and sciences and all peoples and epochs are only branches and twigs of that tree; consequently, they all have only *one course,* the course of nature. As nature proceeds from chaos toward order, from disharmony toward harmony, from disproportion toward proportion, man, likewise, progresses in history toward freedom through slavery, toward truth through error, toward justice through injustice. So also a mature, civilized man passes in his lifetime along the same course which mankind traversed in history thousands of years before him.

Everything tends toward one and *the same goal,* because everything travels one and the same path. In modern times equality is the common end of all historical forces and phenomena. Christianity and Darwinism, press and railway, guns and industry, all urge man in the same direction. Proportion, and even disproportion produce this same effect on all sides. The absence of freedom is always immoral, uneconomical; the immoral and the unreasonable can never be beautiful. Reason, on the other hand, always leads in the direction of reconciliation and love, toward justice and freedom. Beauty awakens and strengthens the moral, the reasonable, the good and truthful. Every real truth is at the same time beautiful, moral and honest, while the false is neither moral nor beautiful, neither good nor righteous. Truth kills that which should not live, the lie kills that which should flourish. To be moral and honest means to love, to search for and to defend the truth. Injustice is error; an unjust society is a false society; every false situation is an unrighteous situation and, accordingly, the extension of truth is the extension of justice.

The *relationships* of nature and the relationships of human life are *one and the same*. All life on earth depends upon the sun, and the life of the human mind in all the regions of sciences on the development of astronomy, for theories and ideas in all other sciences are only the consequences and derivations of astronomical views. The sun stands toward the earth as astronomy stands toward geology; what the earth is to organic life, geology is to biology. Thus, to link the organic beings of the earth to the life of the earth herself is to link the earth's life to that of the sun and of the cosmos, to bind biology to geology and geology to astronomy. The unity of mind is the unity of life. The simpler the subject of a science, the simpler the science itself, and the simpler the history of its subject-matter. The history of astronomy concerns primarily the struggle of two principles—geocentrics and heliocentrics, chaos and harmony. The more

116

complicated the subject of a science, the longer and more complex is its history: the history of man and his mind is the history of everything. All the forces of life, in general, are woven in it, for it is spun from the finest of all life's threads. Thus, all philosophies, religions and sciences stand toward man's mind, as races, tribes and peoples stand toward mankind. Today we are still, in both respects, in a quasi-feudal age of development: there are many independent peoples and many independent sciences. It is in individual sciences that the progress of the human mind occurs, and in individual peoples the progress of mankind. Man's spiritual life cannot be appreciated from the standpoint of one religion, one philosophy, literature or science; the whole man, in all the aspects of his life, can be found only in history, only in mankind. So we may say that philosophical history stands toward ordinary history, preoccupied with personalities and concrete events, as algebra stands toward arithmetic, and higher mathematics toward the lower.

Since that one and great whole grows from a single root, it can *emerge only once and can live only once.*

Since the proper conditions for man's appearance occurred only once on the earth, mankind is only one, lives only once, and passes through history only once. The history of man is, thus, one, and has one beginning. Just as every individual has only once been a child, mankind has passed once, and only once, from the natural savagery to the highroad of history; only once did it pass through the phases of natural life, only once was fire discovered, only once were letters developed from primordial pictures. And precisely because the history of mankind is so unified, precisely because man lives his history only once, whatever

117

happens in history, happens only once. Civilization is becoming more and more unified; it does not begin anew in various places and times.

Since civilization is only one, and has only one existence, there is less and less independence in life and in the purely organic development of the individual civilized peoples; the life of history's later civilizations recedes further and further from the primitive. The threads of man's history become increasingly interlaced, so that the history of one people cannot be understood without the history of other peoples, both past and present. Not one of the modern European peoples passed directly from primitive life to the complexity of modern society; none of them repeated the discovery of fire, tools, agriculture and writing; none has its own original civilization; they are based on classical antiquity. It is only the oriental civilizations that are primary and original; all the others are secondary, derivative, the consequences and results of the first; the original civilizations alone existed in organic harmony with nature. The new peoples [in the Middle Ages] began their history with monotheism, which is the final result of all ancient civilization. The foundation of man's history was laid only once, and all the rest of history is but further building on this one foundation. All the particular peoples of history, both ancient and modern, are unconsciously building one great home for mankind, whose foundation lies deep in the darkness of the primordial, natural life of man. Thus the highest reason is found only in history; it is only from the perspective of the entire history of the universe that one can grasp the whole.

CHAPTER XXIII

All human affairs follow the path of nature, and man discovers and studies phenomena in the same order as they appear in nature. In other words, the natural succession in which things occur is the same as that in which man discovers them and thinks of them.

The sciences appear in history in the same succession as the objects of their observation and study appeared in nature. Nature existed before man, and the natural sciences developed before the social sciences. First astronomy linked the earth to the cosmos, then geology and biology bound man to the earth and to the animal kingdom, and lastly, it remains for history to bind man to man, the natural to the historical. Because man first studied nature, the geocentric error, the error of man about nature, was overthrown before the anthropocentric, the error of man about man. Anthropology has always been the last phase in human thinking and observation. The science of man is still far from reaching the level of exactness and law attained by the natural sciences; while, of course, the study of man's anatomy started earlier and is more advanced than the study of his psyche or his history. Likewise, natural religions are far older than the spiritual ones.

As the inorganic world preceded the organic, the sciences of the inorganic world developed before the others, and the sciences of organic matter are still far from the exactness of the inorganic sciences. The laws of the earth's life were discovered before the laws of organic life; geology as a science is older than biology. Chemical processes began later than physical ones, and chemical science followed astronomy; the mechanics of air was known before its chemistry. As the universe and the sun are older than the earth, knowledge of the sky developed before knowledge of the earth. An understanding of the earth's form developed slowly and late. The first regularity, the first natural law, was found in the sky, and only later in the earth and in her life.

As water was at first mingled with the air, and only later separated from it, so the composition of the air was discovered before that of water.

The laws of space were discovered first, and the first sciences—astronomy and mathematics—were based upon them; the laws of time were developed only later. As electricity and magnetism are the youngest forces of nature, for which we have not developed any special senses, as we have for warmth, light and sound, they were discovered and used later than the others.

Man became acquainted with the earth in the same succession in which her original parts arose from the sea. America and Australia in their physical constitution are the youngest continents, and they were the last discovered by the current of history. The various parts of the earth were inhabited and cultivated by man in the same succession in which they rose above the waters. Asia, the oldest continent, was first settled by man. The earth was uniformly warm before the present climatic zones developed; accordingly, the first cultures appeared and developed in the warm zones. The first civilizations depended, not on climate, but on the soil and its fertility. It was only later that civilization moved toward regions with seasonal variations. Thus, regions of the globe which became the seats of civilizations did so in the same order in which they rose from the seas, and human culture in Asia and Europe followed first their peripheries. The geographical progression, in which the mainlands arose, constitutes, at the same time, the geographical progress of civilization. As the sun first lights the earth's peaks, as consciousness first illuminates elevated individual spirits and from them descends to the depth of society, so civilization first illuminates the highest areas, that is to say, those which first rose from the water, and only then descends to the depths of the continents.

The aristocracy of clergy and warriors are the first social elements to rise above the primitive mass; they rose first to civilization, and were the first to be studied by history; only later was it concerned with the life of the people. Likewise, sociology and economics could not appear and develop before the object of their observation and study—the masses of society—arose.

As weight is the first characteristic noticed in matter, in the history of mankind weight was the characteristic man first recognized and applied; weight was the first stimulus in the liberation of man. Man's first tools had to overcome the force of gravitation. In the first societies, money, and even votes were measured by weight. In the first stages of social life only the votes of those who used to "weigh," in terms of their property, strength or knowledge, mattered; the counting of votes began with democracy. The difficult hieroglyphs preceded the simple letters, and every science begins by attacking the weightiest problems. And in one aspect the whole process of civilization is only an easing of burdens, of weight. Just as language was the first liberation of man's spirit from the burden of external impressions, so man himself became free first from the burden of labor; almost all his physical strain has been taken over by the machine. The first division of labor in society resulted from distinctions as to the strenuousness of work.

Not only do men discover and think and understand things in the same succession in which these appear, but man's senses appear and develop in the same order in which the things and material phenomena observed by the senses appear, and man perceives things with his senses in the same order in which they appear.

Warmth is the first feeling; the sense of seeing develops only after birth, just as heat comes before light. And as sound is only a later manifestation of life, so is the sense of hearing developed later than the senses of warmth and light. Just as the telescope and telegraph were discovered before the telephone, so the silent sundial preceded the ticking clock. Man's eye sees the object first, then recognizes its color, as color is a later attribute of things. Colors were also perceived by man in the same order in which they appeared. Red, the oldest and strongest, was the first to affect the human eye, and after, the yellow; red and yellow are the arch-colors; blue and violet, as the youngest, were noticed last; in the remotest ages they were quite unknown.

Man also shows talent first for those fields of knowledge which are the first to appear—for art and mathematics.

Since proportion is the last phase of the processes

of life, it is also the last thing that man notices in the various aspects of existence, and he attains it last in his society.

Benefit and need were the first stimuli for man's discoveries and studies, and man discovers and studies things in the order in which they become needful to him; study and need succeed in the same order.

The first human necessity, lacked by animals, is fire, and fire was the first discovery of man; printing, steam, electricity, and other things were discovered later, when the need for them appeared. Astronomy was the first science and in the earliest times only astronomy was necessary and useful to man. There was no science more useful than astronomy throughout antiquity, for the sciences of agriculture and navigation were founded on the knowledge of the sky. The basis of the spiritual and religious is astronomy. The need for a science of chemistry was felt long ago, but the necessity for the social sciences and for scientific history is of a later date; it is the need of a riper mind. When the real need for America was unconsciously felt, it had to be discovered. Then was the proper time, and only then could it occupy a useful place in the stream of history.

CHAPTER XXIV

*Since man investigates things in the same suc-
cession in which they appear and become necessary to him, it follows that things appear in the
same succession in which they become necessary,
or, vice versa, things become necessary in the same
succession in which they appear.*

As animals could develop only after oxygen appeared in the atmosphere, that is, when oxygen became necessary, so is warmth, the first physical force
and first necessity, the primary condition of all creation and development. As heat existed when there
was still no air, so man needs for life warmth before
he needs air; and as air exists before water, air becomes, after warmth, the first and strongest need of
animals. And as light is only a result of heat, the need
for light is subsequent to that for heat. The child in
the uterus does not need light. And as only the eye
needs light, while the prior, lower senses can function
as well in darkness, so only the mind needs light.
Since the preservation of life is the first and most
important necessity, the need for reproduction arises
only later [when physical existence is assured].
Likewise, the senses serve primarily for physical
maintenance; as tasting and smelling, so seeing and
hearing are originally only the safeguards of the liv-

124

ing creature. The sharp sense of hearing of primitive man becomes duller with the growth of civilization, as greater security of life renders it unnecessary. Thus, man has senses for warmth and light, but none for electricity; accordingly, heat and light are more essential to man, and, in fact, they became known to man before electricity.

The senses, too, develop in the same succession in which they become necessary, and in which the objects which they discern appear. The sense of touch is the sense of darkness, a dumb sense of warmth, and of the bodily. It is prior to all the rest of the senses, as warmth is the primary condition and the first necessity of everything. It is only later that vision developed, for the need for light occurs later than the need for warmth, just as light developed in the cosmos after heat. In the same way, the sense of taste is older than the sense of smell.

Warmth is the primal necessity and the first condition of human civilization also, so that it was only in the warm regions of the earth that man could raise himself for the first time to civilization. As water is one of the primary necessities of man, the first mechanical force in nature that man discovered, mastered and used was water power. Until the application of steam power, water was the only motive force for major enterprises. Water is the first condition for agriculture and commerce, and, accordingly, for civilization, which first appeared in fertile river valleys. So warmth and water are not only primal necessities for life and development, but also for civilization.

Man is first of all the protegé of Nature, but after Nature, the first necessity of immature mankind is religion; it was under the protection of religion that man cultivated and elaborated all the aspects of his historical life. In a similar way science and literature required the protection of the upper classes until, in very recent times, sufficiently developed, they penetrated the life of the people, where such protection was no longer necessary. As the masses of society rise, the need arises for the goods, which were originally the exclusive property of the upper classes, to become the common goods of all human beings. Accordingly, they must become cheap, must increase, and thus the amount of necessary labor also increases. All economic progress tends toward the increase of production and the cheapness of goods.

At first, reading, writing and education were the needs of only a few, so that the number of educated persons was small, and literature was limited to the upper classes. The necessity for the press and for wider education was felt only when the masses began to rise. The press is a democratic invention; knowledge and more precise views began to expand to ever broader and deeper strata of society only through the press. Printing was discovered only in modern times because only then did it become necessary—not because its inventor happened to be born only then.

Only necessity and usefulness bring about the expansion of consciousness and knowledge; only need and benefit extend the awareness that the highest good of man consists in the good of others, the well-being of all society; that the good of every people is in the good of all other peoples; only the realization of necessity and of reward brings men, peoples and epochs closer and closer to one another. And all the modern developments—science, press, the railway, telegraph, etc.—exert their influence in this direction. Agriculture and commerce are earlier needs than printing, and they developed with the first societies; the press appeared as a need of a later, riper period of history. Every necessity of a later epoch is a luxury for the earlier ones, and is, therefore, unnecessary; and every present luxury is only in the way of becoming a later need, the necessity of a higher and riper age.

At the primary level of historical life man needs only nature, and just as man appeared later than nature, so is man only a later need to man; organized states and societies came into existence only after a long period of natural life. Only as men increased in numbers, only as human needs increased, did the need for others, for society, increase. With the growth of consciousness man comes to realize more and more his need for others, he is directed more and more towards them. And man's need for mankind is still too high and too abstract a requirement to be generally realized; with the ever stronger feeling and need of humanity for itself, the notion of one mankind is beginning to ripen. Mankind emerges ever more visibly from behind the walls of nations, states, races, and tribes. All the factors of modern history are working for the creation of this one mankind, from ocean to press, from science to the common needs of people; the need for one mankind is growing, and one mankind is ever more clearly coming into being. Humaneness, one of the last and thinnest layers of the human mind, is increasing, is developing more and more, as men need one another more, in ever larger numbers; in primitive times it was quite unnecessary.

The need for personal rule and influence preceded the need for law, which came only with a higher level of social life. Accordingly, man's natural affection for human personality is prior to his respect for law; in his life and work man is guided first by personalities and only in riper periods by ideas, for only then does he begin to feel the necessity for laws and principles.

Since the need for society arises after the need for physical maintenance, and since man needs language only in society, it follows that the need for language is, likewise, a later need of man, and this is indeed why it appears later. So in general, it is only after the silent creation of life that the need for sound, expression and speech arises. Just as the earth was originally mute, so, for a long time, the first rituals consisted of silent actions; the hymn developed only later.

Religion is the primary need of the human spirit, and it appeared with the separation of man from the rest of nature. The necessity for science and philosophy began to be felt only with the growing maturity of the spirit, and both of them appear only on the higher levels of historical life. In ancient times religion and slavery made science and industry unnecessary, because science, like all complex things, can only flourish and become useful on a broad and solid foundation, and this foundation was only lately provided with the elevation of the masses and with the press. Since natural requirements are more essential to man than the social, the need for the natural sciences arises before the need for the social ones, and in fact, the natural sciences appeared and developed their laws before the social. As heliocentrics was unnecessary to the ancient mind—in those times it was only necessary to watch the phenomena of nature, and to determine their spatial and temporal relationships, so it was only on the higher, the more mature levels of history that the necessity for more just and righteous social relations, the need for the liberation of men from the pressure of particular incidents of history, appear. These were the compulsions that brought about the development of the social sciences, the study of man's historical and social relations, the investigation of his inner nature and that of society. This is why the social sciences appear much later than the natural.

The scientific value of history as well as the necessity for it grows progressively with the increasing value of and need for time. All the other sciences are preoccupied with the study of things in space; only history studies the life of things in time. The ever ripening spirit of man necessitates an ever better understanding of things and events, and since all that exists is simply the result of a long series of previous phenomena, nothing can be completely understood without a knowledge of its past and prediction of its future. All that exists, exists only within, and develops out of history. For a thing to be understood, its history must be known. With the ever growing need for understanding things and phenomena the need for history grows. The highest understanding can, therefore, be only the historical understanding. As it becomes more and more the only philosophy of the human mind, it continually draws all things into itself, occupying the fields of all the other sciences, and making everything human and earthly, historical. It thus becomes increasingly necessary to all the other sciences; it stands toward them as time to space or as consciousness to unconsciousness.

Architecture satisfies the primal needs of man, both practical and ideal; it is the earliest of all the arts, and it stands toward the other arts as astronomy stands toward the other sciences.

CHAPTER XXV

Not only do things come into being whenever they become necessary, but they last only as long as they are necessary; as soon as they are no longer needed they disappear. And since the total quantity of time available to the living whole is determined and limited, the later a particular phenomenon arises—in other words, the later a thing becomes necessary, the less time there remains to it to exist; the later the necessity for a thing arises, the less time it lasts, the sooner it disappears. Thus the succession of disappearances is reciprocal to that of appearances; the later a thing appears, the sooner it disappears; the earlier a thing appears, the later it disappears; the prior survives the posterior.

In the process of human history all that appears later, that is to say, all that is further removed from the natural condition, disappears, and the whole historical process tends toward an ever closer approach to the natural again, so that, with the lapse of time, there will be less and less of the artificial, the historical and human. Man is more ancient than races, tribes and peoples, man will survive races, tribes, peoples and states; man will be the last link of that historical chain which began with the human species. As custom was the first moral force, the first integrating element in human society, all morality, which was artificially maintained by laws, will be reduced, at last, to custom again, so that law, at the last level of human development, will become unnecessary and disappear.

As in an excessive shock every man loses first his consciousness, his conscious will, so when a people dies, the first things that disappear are its latest acquisitions, its education and intellect, and they disappear first from where they have penetrated last— from the masses. With every civilized people that has lost its independence, education and civilization disappeared first from the lower classes, where they had last penetrated, and the original natural ignorance again enveloped the masses. Language, religion and poetry are the first focal points of a people's ideation, the first expressions of the popular spirit, and when all its other expressions are lost to the people there remains to it only its language, religion and poetry, and in these it continues living its life. Language and poetry, customs and religion survive all the other forms and organizations, which are the later results of its historical life.

This ever growing emancipation from the artificial and historical, this closer and closer approach to the natural in all aspects of life, this larger and better understanding of nature, will lead the spirit of man at last to the original religion, the religion of nature. In primeval times Sun worship was general. The whole development of knowledge brings one to the conviction that the Sun is the source of all life and all forces on the earth; the cult of the Sun will mark the end of conscious science just as it marked the beginning of unconscious religion.

As civilization is only the result of a surplus of human energy, a surplus unspent in the struggle for existence, so is human life in general simply the result of a surplus of the energy of the earth's life. Man, with his society and his civilization, is only a luxury of nature. As the earth's energy diminishes, there will be less and less of it for the maintenance of man, and the loss will be felt first by man and his civilization. The general process of dying and disappearance will begin in man's history and civilization; the earth's pulse will stop beating first in man's civilization and history.

Historical, conscious and civilized man will disappear first, while a wild, natural and unconscious man will long survive civilization and history — the child will survive the man. Unconscious of its history and past, humanity will die in natural savagery and darkness, as in savagery and darkness it was born. Man, the last of earth's creatures, will disappear first of all the earthly things. In all his history man is only a second on the clock of life-in-general.

Since the psychic developed from the more general organic, so in dying the first to disappear is the higher conscious life, then the lower; even in health, psychic energy would soon be dissipated if it were not periodically returned to organic life in sleep. As in the process of sleeping the first thing to disappear is consciousness, the last product of the psyche, as the sense of touch, the first and general sense, remains to man even when all the other senses betray him and help him no longer—so with every stronger shock the later, higher, psychic life disappears first, while the organic continues (breathing, digestion, etc.); and when the body dies, it is breathing that stops first.

Thus, the psychic, as a later development, is the first to return into the organic; later the organic returns into the inorganic, and the inorganic, as the life of the whole will long survive both. On nature's clock the psychic life is a second, organic life a minute, and the inorganic life of matter, all the rest of time.

In human society everything particular developed from the general and will return into it. The human species was originally an all-embracing whole, from which the individual parts, races, tribes and peoples, which are only particular historical forms of man, evolved only later. In the process of the disappearance of these later historical forms racial differences will survive national and tribal differences, as races developed from the original whole of the human species before tribes and peoples. All the forces of modern history are working to eradicate the national and tribal differences among peoples. Thus one humanity will be at the end of the process which began with the human species; the historical process is only the evolution of the human species into *Man*.

Religion is the original source of all the divisions and branches of the human spirit, and the progress of spirit in history tends toward the dissolution of all its particular forms into one common religion. Just as the idea of *Man* will finally unite and reconcile within itself all the individual ideas of races, tribes and peoples, so will the highest historical idea join and reconcile in itself the particular ideas of all the individual religions, philosophies and sciences, and this highest idea will find expression in a universal system of religion.

Belief lies at the basis of all knowledge, and belief becomes the end of all knowledge; belief is everything to man; all things originate in it, and all will return to it; it precedes everything and will survive everything. Ultimately belief absorbs all knowledge, for less and less time is available for verifying all the processes, all

133

the methods and proofs by which one comes to understand the results of research. More and more one can only believe in the results of science; the highest ideas, just as the highest results of all sciences and philosophies, are increasingly becoming matters of simple belief. Since religion is the first form of belief, the first entity of the human spirit to evolve from the general stage of faith, a common religion will be the last form of belief—a form in which all later forms, philosophies and sciences, will disappear. Greek philosophy, for example, grew out of religion, and returned, in its last phases, to religion. Likewise, when a people declines, when its literature, philosophy and science can no longer flourish, then, as with individuals, there remains only religion to light it feebly in the darkness into which it strayed. When, with the Roman state, the entire structure of ancient civilization crumbled into dust, religion remained the sole refuge for civilization, for all the sciences and for all the other acquisitions of the human mind. For generations the clergy were the only guardians of the philosophy and science of the ancients.

In religion itself the first things to disappear are the latest elements, those of cult and dogma, leaving an ever increasing proportion of its most ancient components. Thus, all of Christian religion was reduced to cult which, modified, dates from its remotest beginnings, and to prayer which men used to implore the gods, asking for their gifts, protection and mercy.

So the last phase of the life and development of the particular and individual is to dissolve into the more general, the earlier; individuals die, but societies and peoples survive; and as peoples and states perish, mankind will remain. When an individual man dies, he first stops being a member of his society and people, but in his family he survives much longer, for the family is a much earlier form than society, and it remembers him still when society has long since forgotten.

Society is now the heir to the spiritual achievements of each individual; one day it will be the only heir of his material acquisitions as well. For spiritual achievements are a later development, and they are the first to stop being simply an individual's good, while property and material acquisitions are prior to the spiritual and they will continue much longer to be individual goods.

Originally man was bound to nature in such a way that he did not feel in any way separated from it, and the final end of the entire process of history is the re-approach to nature [on another level]; the unity of the spirit of man to the life of nature is developing more and more.

Man's consciousness is the last result of his internal processes, and in old age, crises and pains, it is the first thing to give way, to disappear into the general unconsciousness, while the unconscious drives and reflexes continue. So it is with life in general: Intellectual abilities weaken and disappear first, while the sense, the emotions, the more primitive elements of the psyche, persist much longer. And, as in the end, all knowledge passes over in belief, all consciousness passes ultimately into unconsciousness; words and actions are being progressively mechanized.

At the time of man's entrance into history, nature affected him by its externals, its forms and its accidents; civilizations first appeared in those regions where external nature was convenient to them. The religious and philosophic ideas of all the ancient peoples depended on external nature; the idea that water is the first and basic principle of everything originated from the religion of the Nile valley, while the idea of the struggle of Light and Darkness arose from the contrasts of Iran and Turkestan. With the ever continuing progress all man's acquisitions, his religious and philosophic ideas depend less and less upon external nature and more and more on its internal life. As the external disappears man is less influenced by it; he emancipates himself from the influence of externality and accident, comes to depend increasingly on the internal life of nature, on earth and sun, and adapts his way of living more and more to the laws of internal nature. Accordingly, there are fewer disturbances and withdrawals, since external and accidental causes are no longer as capable of obstructing social life and development. Thus there is ever less of what is usually called chance and accident, for the life of society is less and less bound to externals. Approaching nature more and more, man is coming into progressively closer relations with it. As inorganic forces—steam, electricity, etc.—increasingly reduce the need for organic forces, man's use of the inorganic resources begins to surpass his use of the organic. The use of coal and iron assured the economic life of society and stimulated the progress of civilization; higher civilization was made possible only through this direct reliance of man on inorganic nature. Nature affects civilization less and less with its secondary and later forces and phenomena, such as the situation of the land, fertility, climate and so on, while it exerts an increasingly greater influence through its earlier, inner forces—coal, and Sun.

Science, as it matures, tends increasingly toward the direct communication with life and its needs, as in the beginning. It tries more and more to be of service to man, while in its youth, its transitional phases, its objective was to rise above life and the needs of life. Likewise, in human society the tendency is toward the establishment of ever more direct relations among people, a task which is being accomplished by modern means of communication.

As laws tend to become custom, and conscious action to become mechanic, so the sciences are again becoming arts and crafts, as they were in the beginning. Realizing better now that man's destiny depends on the sun and stars, and that his life is bound to the general life of the cosmos, astronomy is developing into the craft by means of which one will be able to read the destiny of earth and man from the life of the sun and stars. Serving increasingly life and its needs, chemistry is returning more and more to its original phase: It is becoming the art of assuring better and more stable conditions of life. Art and craft will survive philosophy and science. The traces of man's crafts are the oldest relics of his life, and they will be his last monuments, also. The succession of disappearance is the same in art: When all the other arts were more or less in ruin, architecture lasted as an art until the fall of the Roman Empire.

As in the cosmos, so in human society, the later, smaller phenomena live out their courses faster and perish before the greater, earlier ones. Just as the smaller bodies of the particular classes and tribes disappear into the larger bodies of the peoples, so the great truth of *Man* will survive all the little truths of tribes, peoples and states; history will be reduced ultimately to a few great laws and periods which will dissolve and absorb all the many little personal names, tribes, peoples, events and dates; a few great names and principles will survive all the little names and laws.

Since the light of civilization appears first on the peaks of society, in individual elevated minds, and only then descends into the depths and valleys, it follows from the law of disappearance that civilization and progress will start dying out in the masses of society, where they penetrated last, and that in the end education and civilization will remain only on the peaks, in the minds of elevated individuals, from which they descended in the beginning. The peaks of mankind will still flame in the sunset when darkness and ignorance shall have long since overwhelmed the masses. As the sunlight disappears first from the lowlands, while the mountain peaks still glisten in the light of the setting sun, so when peoples fall, it is only individual spirits that continue to bear the standards of the national ideals; they alone remain the bearers of its history. The light of history still illumes the elevated minds long after it has left the deeps and valleys of society. When Rome declined, science and education continued to be cultivated only by the élite, while superstition and ignorance flooded over the masses; and, as all civilization and literature, so did literary Latin remain alive only among the upper classes. In the same way, in the second period of Hindu literature, Sanskrit remained only the language of the cultivated, the language of literature, while the masses forgot it and spoke a different one. Accordingly, the light of civilization, of consciousness and reason, was born on the eminences of society, and there it will last be extinguished.

* * * * *

As everything appears when it becomes necessary, lasts only while it is necessary, and disappears when the need which occasioned it disappears, it follows that all that disappears is unnecessary, and that there remains only what ought to remain. Everything unnecessary is a luxury which is first to be sacrificed in emergencies. The earth having spent the greatest part of her energy for the creation of the inorganic and the organic worlds, man and civilization are maintained only on the surplus. Man and his civilization, his spiritual life and progress, are merely the luxuries of nature. When the earth's energy begins to diminish, when it becomes necessary to concentrate the disappearing resources at her command, the spiritual life of man and man's civilization will be sacrificed first, as man himself, in his emergencies, jettisons first of all his own spiritual life. The natural man, with his natural needs, will long survive civilization and history, these luxuries of his long existence.

Thus, everything which appeared in time will in time disappear; all things born must die. Only that which never began will never end; that which preceded everything else will survive everything else; that which appeared first will disappear last.

PART II

THE LAW OF
PROPORTION
IN HISTORY

CHAPTER I

*It is apparent from the law of succession that
things develop, separating from the great general
whole, in the same order in which they become
necessary; accordingly, everything which develops
earlier represents an earlier and more important
necessity; all things which develop later are progressively less necessary. The necessity of things
is proportional to their priority in time.*

1. Because of its size, energy, heat and light, the
Sun is the most necessary thing for all the planets and
for all inorganic, organic and psychic life. For man as
well, the earlier inorganic phenomena are much more
necessary for food, social life, civilization and progress than the later, organic ones.

Man's greatest need is for food, and the means of
obtaining it are more necessary than all other things;
the products of agriculture are more necessary than
any other products. The needs of the body are prior
to all other needs; they are much more strongly felt
than those of the spirit. All man's spiritual forces developed only in the service of the body, especially of
the stomach. Man must spend the greatest part of his
physical and spiritual energy for the satisfaction of
bodily needs—food, clothing and so on. Thus, only
the surplus of man's energy can be used for the satisfaction of later, spiritual needs, which disappear, like

every other luxury, whenever the preservation of physical life absorbs all his strength.

The earliest elements of civilization—fire, weapons and tools—are the most necessary. The family, the first form and phase of every sort of later and higher society, is a much stronger need of mankind than any other form of companionship. The family satisfies man's first and most urgent needs; it has been the basic need of every historical community, while the need for people, state and society is only a later, higher, and therefore lesser, need of mankind.

Religion is more necessary to society than are science and philosophy; being concerned more with man's emotions than with ideas, it is necessary to a larger part of man's mind than are the other two. Likewise, architecture satisfies always and everywhere the most important needs of man, whereas all the other arts satisfy later, and therefore less important needs.

Astronomy was the most necessary and most useful science, not only in ancient times, where it appeared before all the other sciences, but it has remained and always will remain the most useful of all, for the laws of all the others rest upon the laws of astronomy.

2. Accordingly, the earlier a thing appears, the more value and significance it has for things which succeed it, and the later it comes, the less significance it has. The stone does not need sunlight, but the sunlight is necessary for plants and essential for man. And of all the parts of man's nature, his spirit requires light most of all.

3. *Since the prior is necessary to all the posterior, it follows that the posterior is less necessary, is not necessary to anything prior to itself. The lack of necessity in things is reciprocally proportional to their priority in time.*

144

Organic life is not necessary for the maintenance of the inorganic; air, water and earth do not need plants and animals; plants do not need animals or man; and man, the latest phenomenon of the general process, is not necessary to anything prior to himself—not to the animals, the plants, the air, earth or sun. All these phenomena, being prior to man, can exist as well without him. Man and his mind are simply unnecessary to everything that appeared and developed before he did. Man is necessary only to man, and to nothing else. Moreover, man is man's least need, because the latest. All the other, prior things—air, water, vegetation and so on—are more necessary to man than is the company of his fellows. Man is the most unnecessary thing in the general process of life; he is the greatest of earth's luxuries. Insofar as Nature is concerned with man at all, it maintains only the organic in him, only man the brute; all his later, higher needs, all his higher life, he must maintain by himself.

4. Since later phenomena need all the preceding ones, it follows that *the earlier a thing is, the fewer contingencies it has, and the later it is, the more.*

Man, the latest element of the general process, needs all the preceding developments; and therefore, he has more needs than any thing prior to himself. He needs all the elements, forces and phenomena of the inorganic world; he needs warmth and light, air and water, plants and animals. And in his earlier ages, the more primitive he was, the fewer needs he had; original and ancient man did not need many things which are indispensable for his modern offspring— the printing press, railways, electricity, dynamite, the telegraph; the latter, the higher the man, the more needs he has. Moreover, with the progress of his reasoning ability, the necessity for all the things that exist, or that have existed, or that will exist, is realized more and more.

So the earlier a thing is, the more needed it is, and the fewer needs it has, while the later it appears, the greater is the number of its needs, and it is needed, in turn, by fewer and fewer things.

5. Since the prior is more necessary, everything prior has ever increasing value and significance for progressively later developments. Just as the first, the beginning stage of the earth determined all her later development, so the childhood of man is of primal importance to all his later progress. Then it is that man acquires the basis for all later evolution of his mind and spirit. The child's first impressions are most significant for all his later life; they are the basis for all further advancement of his psyche. The germs of the feelings, inclinations and dispositions which man brings with him into the world determine the development of all his later character, and ultimately, therefore, the broad outlines of his destiny. In the same way, language, the first and most important creation of man, lies at the foundation of all his historical progress, since it is only by means of language that an individual can inherit all the acquisitions of the preceding epochs. Language introduces man into the family, into society, and into the history of the whole genus.

So the first epochs of history, with the first steps on the road of social development, the first discoveries, inventions and crafts, man's first perceptions and ideas, are far more significant than all the later ones.

6. *The earlier a thing is, the more value and significance it has, and the less replaceable it is; the later it is, the more easily can it be replaced.*

Just as the family cannot be replaced by any state

institution or any other higher form of historical society, while it can replace all the later and higher forms of social organization, so religion cannot be replaced by any science or philosophy, while it constitutes a sufficient compensation for these latter to the masses of every society. In general, faith always compensates for insufficient knowledge and an impotent mind. A people does not fall when it loses its state, its laws, literature or science; it falls when its family deteriorates, when it loses its language, customs and religion. Man can exist even when he loses the power of reasoning.

CHAPTER II

As the prior is necessary to the posterior, every-
thing posterior depends upon the prior; every-
thing prior is the condition of the posterior. Since
the prior does not need the things that come after
it, it follows that the earlier a thing, the fewer
conditions it has, while the later it is, the more
conditions there are. The independence of things
is proportional to their priority in time; their de-
pendence is proportional to their lateness in time.

The earth, with her inorganic, organic and spiritual
life, depends upon the sun, upon the quantity of the
heat and light she receives, upon the velocity of her
revolutions. Similarly, the later, organic life depends
on many more conditions than the earlier, inorganic.
It needs sunlight and heat; it is subject to the structures and combinations of the inorganic world, to
geographic location, climate and moisture. Thus,
plants depend on much fewer conditions than animals, which, being later, depend also on plants.

Accordingly, man, the latest and highest phenomenon on earth, depends in his own existence and progress upon all that appeared and developed before
him.

The warmth of the sun is the primary condition of
man's life, and of his civilization and progress, but his
natural and historic existence depends also upon all
the other inorganic and organic forces and

phenomena. Man's first works, his first societies and their organization, his ways of life, the first forms of his beliefs, notions and cultures, his first customs and migrations—all depended on external nature: on climate, geographical situations, seas, rivers, mountains and plains; on vegetation and the fertility of the soil; on the distribution, abundance and direction of the waters; on the atmospheric moisture and the means of subsistence; in other words, the first civilizations depended upon the convenient places and regions of the earth.

The life and the possibility of man's mind and spirit are conditioned not only by his general physical organization, which is the product of the preceding forms, of the size, distribution and proportion of the organs and of their functions, but also of his erect posture. This erect posture freed his arms and his vision, and is the condition of all man's progress in history. It is the source of the power of his mind and spirit. The freed vision, resulting from the erect posture, gave rise to the first human language, which in turn forms the basis for every human society.

Man's mind and spirit likewise depend on bodily uniformity, and only because his body has remained unchanged throughout historical times, and with it the basic forces of his psyche, was social heredity possible. And this latter is the base upon which all progress is built, for it is only by transmission from generation to generation of man's acquisitions and powers that these may be preserved, multiplied and developed. If man's body and soul had changed in various historical epochs, he would have had to begin living anew after each change, since, along with his body, his basic desires, inclinations and abilities would likewise have changed.

And the body with its organs and their functions does not depend at all upon man's will or mind; breathing, nutrition, circulation and secretion do not in the least depend on man's thinking and consciousness.

Emotions and their strength, which all animals and man share, depend upon the physical organization, and all the later forces of the psyche depend upon the strength of the emotions. Feeling is the starting point of all other psychic processes. The strength or intensity of feeling determines the strength of belief, and upon this depend activity and strength of will. The power of presentation depends on the intensity of emotion, and in turn conditions the ability to understand. For example, the sense of hunger is the first and basic condition for the possibility of and necessity for working, and all man's progress is based on labor. Similarly, the senses, the organs of the mind, are bound to the body and depend upon it; the acuteness of the senses conditions the later psychic processes. Sensibility is the primary condition for all knowledge; it must develop before thought can develop; the ability to think and to understand is conditioned by the constitution of the senses. If the senses were not limited there would be no limitation to man's consciousness. Thus, limitation of the senses permits the interruption of the continuity of feeling and thereby enables man to know and to distinguish. All of man's knowledge and understanding depends upon that limitation of his senses. The hearing of the blind is less dispersed and penetrates the psyche more deeply, so that all impressions entering his mind through hearing are much deeper and stronger; among many peoples the blind were the first to awake and cultivate national feelings, ideas, and strivings; they were the first folk poets and bards.

The eye and the ear are the prerequisites for the development of language, which is, in turn, the foundation of human society. Language and reason developed from observation and realization of differences. To understand means to see far below the sensual crust of things; thus, thinking is really seeing. The ability to see and observe is the basis for all religion, sciences and arts (except music); in all the sciences the eye is the sense organ of the highest value.

Not only do mind and spirit depend upon the senses, but among the senses themselves the development, composition and acuity of all other senses depend upon the skin, the sense of touch, the oldest organ of perception.

The highest forces of the mind—reason and consciousness—depend upon all its earliest constituents, as well as upon all the prior forces and phenomena in the history of man and nature. The intellect depends on belief, the fundamental condition of knowledge and understanding, for without belief there could be neither religion nor philosophy, neither science nor society. Reason depends on the intensity of the emotions, on the acuity of the senses, and on language, for truly abstract thinking is not possible without words and language. Language awakened reason, and is the basis and condition of its development. The intellect also depends on bodily organization which is the product of remote historical times. Accordingly, it depends also upon life in general and the composition of earth and sun, on its warmth and light. The intellect depends upon the historical level of society, on time and history, for all ideas are fruits of the tree of history, and ripen only when their time comes. Thus the human mind, the last thing in the succession of universal development, is the last and most complicated result of all the numerous earlier conditions, forces, phenomena, stages, things and processes, and depends, therefore, upon all of them.

Likewise, neither his existence, development, body nor mind depend upon man's consciousness, nor does the life of nature; nothing that occurs or exists depends upon the consciousness of man.

Human economy is the foundation of all society, and all later, higher social forms depend upon the nature and level of economic life. All political and social life depends on the quality and quantity of labor. The increase in labor power, together with a more righteous distribution of the burden of toil, brings about progressively increasing freedom and justice in society and, accordingly, ever greater morality. Higher levels of economy require the expansion of science and education into ever larger circles of society. Increasing populations result in a growing need for ever larger quantities of commodities which can be produced only through increasing technical and scientific development. Thus, not only freedom, justice and morality, but the spiritual level of society as well, depend on the level of the economy; without material well-being there can be no knowledge, education or science.

The strength and the level of all later political and social life depends upon the purity and strength of the family relationship, the basic form and unit of all human society. The disintegration of the family has always been the primary cause of the weakness of society and people, and ultimately of their disintegration as well. Since the feminine principle is, in general, prior to the masculine, it follows that the purity, level and strength of all higher societies depend upon its women (who are the basis of the family); on the quality of the woman, on her body and soul, her health and strength, her upbringing and education, her purity and dignity, depend the structure and form, the strength and level, not only of the family, but of all the other human organizations—of peoples, states, and of mankind itself.

All communication between man and man, and accordingly the possibility of social organization, of tradition and heritage, in other words, the possibility of history, progress and civilization, are based on one of the first goods of mankind—language—without which there would be no knowledge, no science or reason.

The first phase of religion, the belief in the power of the forces of nature over man, determined all the later phases of man's beliefs in science and philosophy, and the belief in the power of man and of his mind. Thus, the level of opinions and ideas in science and philosophy depends upon the level of religion, while religion itself depends neither on science nor on philosophy: it precedes them and therefore does not depend upon them. The final goal of science and philosophy is becoming ever more clearly to render justice to things and people, to determine ever more precisely their value, to ascertain ever more accurately the measure and limits of all natural and social phenomena. This goal of the sciences and of philosophy was determined by religion, which established the belief in one, righteous god of all men and things—a single creator of everything. The longing of the intellect for unity, the endeavor of science and philosophy to explain all phenomena by one single force was determined by religion, by the belief in one God. The notion of law and of the regularity of nature could not develop from a belief in the struggles of many capricious gods. The lower the level of religion, the lower the man and the society and the less there is of truth, justice and freedom.

Just as the life of the earth depends upon the sun, so does the level of development of the human mind depend upon the advancement of astronomy. As the first science, astronomy is the prototype of all the other, later sciences: regularity penetrates from the sky into the life of the earth, into organic life, as well as into the life of man in society and in history. The ideas of motion and development could not appear as long as the earth was believed to be fixed.

History, the last of all the sciences, depends upon them all; it requires the greatest number of conditions for the history of mankind to rise to the level of science. In order to understand historical man it is necessary first to understand the physical and psychological man; it is necessary to comprehend his entire inner nature, and the whole of external nature as well. All the forces which affect man from within and without, in all times and places have to be understood; that is, *the historian must understand everything.* In order to untangle one single thread of man's history one must descend down through the strata of the entire history of mankind to the level of the organic and inorganic life; the comprehension of even the smallest modern phenomenon requires a knowledge of all past history. The history of mankind is the last and most complex result of the whole process of life and of all natural forces; accordingly, if one would know man's history, he must know and understand the whole history of nature.

Thus man and his mind depend upon everything that appeared and developed before him, while nothing prior to man depends on him.

Since the internal life is prior to the external, all the external visible and sensible depends upon the structure of the internal; the form depends upon the content; forms are merely expressions, symbols of the inward and invisible, as the shape of the skull depends upon the structure of the brain.

The length of the earth's life, the duration of her existence as a separate body, the number of her rotations and revolutions, the length of the life of everything she bears, depend on the amount of time it took her to separate from the sun, after the first planets; her distance from the sun also depends upon the point in time at which she separated from it, and this distance conditions the speed of her revolutions and rotations, which in turn determine the life span of everything on earth—of plants, animals, and man, and man's society and mind. The amount of heat and light the earth receives from the sun also depends on the distance that separates them, while the quantity and quality of everything on earth, including man's mind, depend on that quantity of sunlight and warmth. A little more or less of both would change the life and form of all earthly things.

Not only does the prior condition everything that follows it; it also conditions the understanding of succeeding things. No thing posterior can be understood out of the context of the prior; one cannot understand man if one does not understand first the life and forces of nature. Thus, since one can understand neither the present nor the future without the understanding of the past, time is becoming increasingly necessary for understanding things and their distribution in space; accordingly, history, the science concerned with the laws of time, is becoming ever more necessary for all the other sciences.

CHAPTER III

Since the posterior depends on the prior, every-
thing which is prior, must, as the condition of the
posterior, already exist, be matured and prepared;
and for the prior to become a stable basis of the
things that follow, it itself must stop developing,
changing and progressing. Accordingly, the ear-
lier attains the limits of its development and
progress sooner than the later.

The soil and the continents, the carriers of man's
history and civilization, achieved their present
makeup long ago; the quantity and the quality of
natural objects are permanently determined; they can
neither increase nor decrease; natural objects and
forces have already achieved their proper places and
act with their proper strength.

Man's body is an earlier phenomenon than his
mind, and stops developing before the mind does; the
body develops and matures faster, and among animals maturation occurs much more rapidly than
among men. Man's childhood lasts much longer than
that of all the other animals. And like the body, the
brain, too, matures much sooner among the animals
than among men. Taken historically, man's body
ripened long before his spirit; even in prehistoric
times man had achieved his physique and has not
progressed physically since those times. Man's body,
the strength, distribution and proportion of his or-

gans, is no longer changing, but his implements and tools are developing further and further and thereby increasing the powers of his limbs and organs.

Thus, the human species matured physically long before the later mankind. Humanity is still growing; it has not yet reached the limits of its physical development. The primary force which created the races, varieties of mankind, has long ceased its activity, while the later, historical force which creates peoples is active even today.

Similarly, the soul of the animal stops growing and progressing and ripens at an earlier age than that of man. The animal is born almost as mature and clever as it needs to be for its entire life, or it only takes a short time to ripen, while man must learn long and hard. Likewise, primitive man reached the limits of the development of his mind and spirit more quickly than historical, civilized man; the same applies to the comparison of earlier peoples with later ones.

Since no individual animal ever escapes the limitations of the soul of its genus, no animal ever attains individuality; no animal can accumulate individual experiences and improve its soul and spirit beyond the limits of its genus; the soul of the genus is achieved, and the soul of any animal stays forever on that level; not rising above the instinct, soul and cleverness of the genus, the soul of the animal stops growing and progressing; the instinct always stays at the same level.

Man's natural, animal impulses, his basic, primitive feelings, longings, and dispositions have remained fundamentally unchanged through all the thousands of years of his historical life; they stopped progressing long ago; only those later forces of his spirit, opinions and ideas are still constantly growing, changing and progressing. Accordingly, all of man's progress in history, all the changes in political and social life depend on changes in thoughts and ideas; it is only through reason that man is acquiring greater and greater control over nature and over himself; it is only reason that introduces justice and freedom among men. There is no other force that can change man, since no other force within him changes, since human nature remains basically unaltered through all the epochs of history. Only progressing reason brings progress in justice, freedom and truth, which are the highest goods of man.

The great majority of people, not rising to the spirit, and inheriting only the acquisitions of the genus, the body and mind, remain on the level of the genus; and as the body and mind are completed sooner than the spirit, the great majority of men quickly stop progressing; they attain very early the limits of their potentialities. So the history and progress of mankind are not, in fact, the work of man, but of the spirit, not of the human species, but of the species *thinker*. And, since the masses of historical mankind are simply the sedimentation of primitive, prehistoric society, all that holds good for primitive man is also applicable to the masses of modern communities. Primitive man develops and matures more rapidly, attains sooner the limits of his capabilities than does historical man. This is why neither primitive society nor the masses of historical societies create or participate in history.

Work, one of the later goods of man, has grown uninterruptedly throughout historical time, while soil, his earliest and most primitive possession, has limits which are already determined.

CHAPTER IV

Since the earlier reaches the limits of its poten-
tialities more quickly, and persists longer in an
unchanging state, the earlier is more stable and
less changing than the later; the later a thing, the
more capable it is of change and progress over a
longer period of time. Stability of things is propor-
tional to their priority in time; changeability of
things is proportional to their posteriority in time.

Nature in general is prior to man and is much less subject to change than he is. Various tribes, peoples and states have appeared and disappeared on earth while her mountains, seas, and rivers have not changed greatly since man developed. The air, the clouds and the stars, as well as the interior of the earth remain unchanged, however much man may strive to change and reshape her surface.

The primary elements and forces of the psyche, those directly bound to the living body and to its needs, remained, like the body itself, basically unchanged through all the epochs of man's history. Fear and rage, love and hatred, all the elementary affects and emotions, are basically the same in both natural and historical man. The impulses to preserve the self and to reproduce are inborn, and therefore unchangeable; moral and intellectual attributes are acquired, later developed, and, accordingly, changeable. So the largest, most stable and least changeable

160

part of man's psyche is shared with the animals, while the region of the intellect, the smallest part of man's mind, which develops last and is spun from the finest threads which are easily tangled and broken, has the longest and most complicated history.

The image of a thing is prior to the idea formed of it, and the idea is much more plastic than the image. (For example, the image of fire has never changed, while the idea of fire has undergone many alterations.)

It is only with the higher, historical man that there can be progress, since the natural, animal type of man remains, with his characteristics and abilities, quite unchanged through all time, settling in the course of development into the masses of the historical societies. And, just as the changes in man's mind occur only in the more highly developed regions, in the spirit and intellect, while the lower, more primitive layers of the psyche remain unaffected, so do all social changes occur only in the higher strata; only the upper levels change and make progress and history, while the masses of every society and of every epoch remain basically the same; they do not make progress or history.

The oldest elements of language have not undergone alteration since the beginning. Pain and pleasure, fear and rage, sorrow and joy have been expressed in all times by the same gestures and interjections, the same mimicry—only the words have changed.

The internal, the earlier, also stays the same; it is only the external that changes. Always and everywhere man has remained basically the same; at all times and places he has the same physical and fundamentally the same psychic organization; all [real]

161

differences among men are merely external and historical. Only the later, only the historically acquired, the external, changes in man; what is within him does not change. Man as an animal will never change any more; only the historical man will change according to the times in which he finds himself.

Likewise, the need for and the value of a thing is less subject to change the earlier the thing appears. The later it develops, the more subject are its necessity and value to alteration. Every man in every age needs air and food, warmth and light; the need for these primary things has never changed, either in quality or in quantity, but the need for learning, science and other later developments changes with the times. The need for and value of fire and tools, as prior, has always remained; yet there were times when railways, printing presses and telegraphic systems were unnecessary.

CHAPTER V

*All earlier things attain more rapidly the limits
of their possibilities and are less contingent upon
other things; they are not readily disturbed by the
later developments; thus prior things come sooner
to regularity and harmony than do later
phenomena.*

The most complete regularity and the most precisely predictable phenomena are found among the
primary things—the celestial bodies, whose motions
are most regular and most precisely defined. The inorganic world displays much more regularity than
does the world of plants and animals. Precise mea-
surements and numbers cannot yet be applied to the
phenomena of the organic world. Their lives, growth,
duration, size, weight and so on cannot be so accurately defined as can inorganic phenomena. And the
further one progresses from the inorganic world toward the organic, and from plants and animals toward man, and from the natural man toward the increasingly civilized, the less he will find of regularity
and obedience to natural law. For the higher forms of
life are woven from ever more numerous and ever
smaller threads, which are always becoming more easily snarled and broken. In nature there are no such
evils, pains, struggles and stresses as are found in
human society.

163

Man sooner attains the physical regularity of the body than the harmony of the mind, and sooner *that* than the harmony of his thoughts.

The earlier an art, the more precise it is, the more subject it is to mathematical regularity. The works of architecture are more regular than those of any other art, and the earlier sciences are more regular than the later, and are subject to more precise laws. Since the earlier is also larger than the later, the larger a thing is, the sooner it attains regularity, and the sooner man becomes aware of it. Hence, regularity and obedience to natural laws in society can only be seen in great intervals of time and space, and only when large measures and numbers are used.

Since proportion is the most necessary condition of regularity, everything that is earlier becomes proportional earlier. The earlier contains fewer elements and parts and therefore attains harmony, definition and proportion among its components sooner than the later. Accordingly the highest degree of proportion, harmony and obedience to law was long ago attained in external nature.

Since proportion is the primary requisite of consciousness and reason, and since the earlier sooner achieves the highest degree of proportion, *early things are more easily understood than things which develop from them; they sooner come to man's attention, are sooner subjected to the laws of reason, and more rapidly attain the level of truth than do later things.* Man became acquainted with the laws of the cosmos long before he knew those of the earth; the intellect could understand and explain the phenomena of the inorganic world in terms of natural law before it could account for those of the organic, and it came upon the laws of the organic world before it found those of the social and historical life of man.

164

CHAPTER VI

Since the posterior depends upon the prior, and accordingly what goes before determines the entire course of what is to come, it follows that the earlier things develop, the more powerful they are, the greater is their influence on all that appears later.

Let us leave, for the moment, the consideration of the sun with its multiple and profound influences on the earth and on all earthly things, and neglect the effect of the great forces of the inorganic world on all organic phenomena, in order to state that the geographic structure of the earth's surface with its inorganic forces predetermined the whole development of the historical life of man. From the geographic structure of the earth one can read the basic traits, one can weave into a fabric the elemental threads of the history of man. The peculiarities of the earth's structure, her phenomena and forces, impressed the characteristic traits on the mind and spirit of the first, natural groups of men, which later determined to a great extent the spirit of all the succeeding peoples of history. The first religious ideas, the first opinions of man concerning himself and the world, which became the basis for all later thought, developed at first, under the direct influence of external nature, of the sun, moon and stars, of light and darkness, heat and cold, fertility and barrenness. The struggle with nature is the basis of all other struggles of man; all the ethical and social struggles, all the internal conflicts, are only derivations of man's primitive struggle with nature and with the natural and bestial elements in himself.

Physical life is the basis of all spiritual life; the needs of the body are the awakeners of spirit and reason. The needs of the body are more irresistible than those of the spirit; the need for food is the strongest stimulus to all of man's progress; it is hunger that makes man work, and labor is the basis of all the development of the human spirit and of man's entire civilization. In the struggle with hunger, all the later, higher and weaker elements of the soul—humanness, love, and so on—recede and withdraw.

The strongest human traits are man's animal characteristics; the animal needs of man are much stronger, more urgent and more enduring than the later, spiritual ones. The natural impulse of self-preservation determines much more strongly man's destiny, his movements and relations, than does the later social sense, and may quite engulf the later, higher and weaker feelings—honor, duty, faithfulness, etc. Egoism is the most powerful motive in the activity and interests of the enormous majority of human beings.

Prior to and more powerful than any other spiritual forces, the instinct affects and determines them creatively. It is the source and stimulus of the rationalized will. The greatest and most noble works of man are stimulated and begun much more under the control of instinct than under that of conscious will, which must itself follow the paths laid out by instinct.

The sense organs are much more developed and affect life more profoundly than the organs of the higher psychic life, as in the brain itself those parts which deal with sensation are more strongly developed and act more powerfully than the parts which perform higher functions. In the same proportion stands the power of feeling to the power of the spirit. Feeling impregnates and moves the whole soul of man and shakes it to much greater depths than the reason is able to. All the greatest and most significant works of mankind were created by the depth and strength of feeling rather than by conscious reason. Not only is feeling much stronger than thinking in the mind of an individual man, but also in every human society it is feeling rather than reason which directs the enormous majority of men. Only emotions can give to thought the strength it requires to influence people. As the enormous majority of human beings live emotionally, and as they are much more strongly affected by emotions than by rational ideas, the only ideas which can move the masses flow directly from and are strengthened by the feelings; ideas which have to do with human emotions, with man's strivings, desires, hopes and interests—in a word, ideas which are religious, political, social or ethical. The influence of scientific and philosophical ideas, on the other hand, is always restricted to the narrow circle of people of spirit and reason. Since emotion changes thinking and ideas, only emotions can clear the way for the expansion of knowledge and enlightenment. Emotion is likewise the source of all poetry, art and religion, and always remains their strongest element. As every truth first appears in the form of obscure feeling and anticipation, and is then illumed by conscious reason, so right and wrong, justice and injustice are first felt, and act first as feelings, before they become clarified and pure ideas.

Among the emotions it is the more elemental, lower

and physical which most strongly affect the body and the functioning of its organs as well as man's life in general—much more so than the esthetic, ethical and intellectual ones.

Thus the most primordial of all feelings—the sensation of *pain*—is the most powerful and intensive of all; pain is the first force which awakens the mind, and only through pain is the *self* strengthened to the highest degree. Pain is the source and foundation of religion; pain awakened man's fantasy, and remained the wellspring of his poetry. Like poetry, every great philosophy developed as a result of the painful impressions of the external world on the spirit of man. Just as physical pains, arising from physical needs, forced man to study things around him, and to search pain and evil for their causes and cures, so the social sciences developed only under the direct pressure of social ills and evils. Only those search for the good and beautiful, the just, the righteous and the true, who suffer from evil and ugliness, from injustice and falsehood.

The power of the senses is much stronger than the power of abstraction, and the sensual side of human nature is much more strongly developed than its spiritual aspect. Sensual pleasures and needs are more powerful, and move man more strongly than do the later, spiritual ones. And among the senses, the sense of touch, the earliest, communicates the most intensive and deepest feelings, the strongest pleasures and the sharpest pains, while in the higher and later senses, the passionate strength and warmth of feelings become less intense. The senses strike up our first acquaintance with the world, and sense impressions and perceptions are the first and strongest materials which enter into the development of the spirit.

Just as the image loses the strength and liveliness of perception and sensation and becomes an increasingly clearer picture in consciousness, so does thinking develop only on the basis of the faded pictures in consciousness. Thinking is the last, and therefore the weakest activity of the spirit, and thus is most easily disturbed by sensations, presentments and perceptions. Presentments are a later phenomenon than sensation and perception, and the weaker and feebler they are, the less trace they leave in the mind: The primary psychic development determines all later relations. The first opinions and ideas of primitive men strongly affect the opinions and ideas of all later times; modern notions and ideas developed only under the powerful influence of oriental and classical thoughts.

Belief, as the first form of the free, conscious reason, created the highest ideas and principles and made the greatest inventions and discoveries; it is the foundation of all the progress of the human mind; belief alone created the great things of history; only profound conviction leads and strengthens the great spirits in the creation and realization of their plans and concepts, ideas, inventions and discoveries.

The first individualization of that primitive, general belief is religion, the awareness of an external world, separated from man and belief in the power of the forces and phenomena of that external world over man. And religion, as it is prior to science and philosophy, is more powerful than they in all epochs of human life, and exerts a mighty influence on all social and individual experiences. By sanctifying custom, the first and strongest tie of social life, religion became the basis for all the higher development of state and society. Indeed, in the first states, all political power derived from the gods, and in all times religion has been the primary and most powerful link between particular communities, cities and tribes, binding them into the larger wholes of state and nation. In the Middle Ages the church was the main spiritual tie among peoples. Religion handed down the first social regulations and laws; through ancient times religion was the sole source of legislation; it alone could give to law the necessary authority, because all laws had to receive divine sanction in order to be respected. In this way, religion also determined the first rights of men, societies, families, peoples and states.

As religion affects both feeling and thinking, as the large majority of human beings in all societies and epochs are more subject to emotions than to thought, religion was the only ideal, historical force which could affect the masses of society, which could move them and lift them to a higher level of understanding and morality. This is why only religious and ethical movements were able to stimulate political and social ones—Buddhism, Christianity, Islam, the Reformation. Religious freedom strongly stimulated the later development of political and social freedom among the European peoples.

Religion likewise lifted and stimulated the material culture of peoples. In all antiquity religion protected and stimulated commerce and communication among men, tribes and peoples. At first commerce could only be carried on near the temples, which gave it safety by their holiness. Religion awakened man's artistic spirit by awakening his aspiration toward the sublime and noble; in all epochs it has been the most powerful stimulus for the development of all the arts. Religion was the first content of the arts of all peoples; it was the inspiration for all higher architecture, as it has always and everywhere stimulated the first poetry. And as it is the basis for epic and lyric poetry, so likewise it is the source of drama among all peoples and in all times.

Religion is the foundation for all education and enlightenment; temples were the first centers of all education and culture; the priests were the first possessors of knowledge, the first scribes. The Protestants, compelled to preach to the people in their own live tongue, raised vernacular languages to organs of national literatures and sciences, and paved the way also for the spiritual elevation and general enlightenment of the people.

So religion, the earliest and most powerful force of the human spirit, became the basis for all later historical acquisitions and opened the first pathways for all human progress.

The idea of beauty, being the earlier and more primitive, awakens and stimulates the later ideas of good and truth and, as an older force, moves men more deeply than the other two. Poetry has been in all ages one of the most powerful forces of history, and poets were the first to awaken national consciousness. Song has always been the most potent force in the introduction of ideas and opinions to the people, and the primary outlet for a people's grief and discontent. When all other means fail, poetry remains the mightiest guardian and conservator of national character, national consciousness and national history. The original union of religion and poetry proved so soul-warming, so stimulating to the human spirit, that it continues to the present day; certain parts of all religious ceremonies have to be sung.

Of all man's powers the latest—consciousness—is the weakest of all, and the creative part of consciousness is the most restricted of all. All of man's historical creations and acquisitions are solely the products of the unconscious. All the great inventions and discoveries in history occurred unwittingly and, therefore, seemingly by accident. All great ideas are conceived in the unconscious activity of the spirit. Since all the great creations of history are products of the unconscious, the first language, the primary and therefore most powerful tool of the intellect, the strongest foundation and precondition for human history and the whole progress of the human mind, also developed unconsciously. Language made possible tradition, the inheritance of the acquisitions of the spirit; it made possible continuity in time without which human history and progress could neither be imagined nor understood. Language is the precondition of poetry, philosophy and science, and of human society, for without it these would be impossible.

Man's first inventions and discoveries—fire, tools, language, poetry, metallurgy, agriculture, and the like—determined and conditioned all the later life of mankind. They were the most potent of stimuli for man's progress; they are the foundations of human history.

Having embraced all prior events as *past*, history powerfully determines the lives of all individuals and peoples, and of all mankind: Its power grows steadily from century to century and from day to day. It is the foundation of all civilization, for it was in the past that all the first and most important steps on the path to progress were made; and it was in the past that mankind's course and destiny were laid out. All civilization and progress are possible only through the inheritance of the past; the roots of all ideas lie buried in the depth of time; they can be received only as a legacy of history.

As for science, each one affects human life and its fellow sciences, the more strongly the earlier it appeared and developed in time, that is, the earlier its subject matter came into existence. Accordingly, as for the strength of influence on all human affairs, *astronomy* is the most important. All the other sciences developed only on the basis of astronomical laws, just as the earth herself derives from the sun the necessary heat and light, as well as the laws of her own life and of the life of everything upon her. Since astronomical laws are prior to, and thereby more potent than, all earthly laws, they expand over those of all the other sciences, just as the sky expands over all the earth. As long as the earth was thought fixed at the center of the universe it was maintained that peace and fixity likewise existed in all the other regions of life, even in human society. When the earth stopped being the center of the universe, man, together with all other things, received a more precise position in the world. The idea that the earth is not fixed, but that it moves around the sun, introduced the idea of motion into all the other regions of life, including human society. It was only on the basis of that idea of movement that the concept of evolution and progress could develop; as long as the earth seemed quiet, no motion or progress was perceived in any area of her life, natural or human. The understanding that astronomical phenomena were subject to law likewise brought about a search for law in all earthly matters, including human affairs.

While the natural sciences, as prior, strengthen man's power over nature and affect all the aspects of human life, the power and influence of the later, social sciences are limited to human society, and they can change relationships only within it. By doing so, they introduce and affirm an ever-growing justice among men.

Thus, since the characteristics and abilities of primitive, natural man are stronger than those of the social individual, everything that is primitive and natural in man is also stronger than that which is later, social and historical—than humaneness, nobility and spirit. Hence, selfishness is stronger than generosity, and the selfish interests of individuals, classes and peoples are always stronger and more decisive than common, higher interests.

Since man's natural needs create all human society, economic life is the basis of all the ensuing forms, both social and political. The form and level of economic life determine the form and level of political life, the degree of historical development. The distribution of the natural and social rights of men depends only on the level of economic development which is the basis and condition of the development of justice in society.

Among economic forces themselves, the earlier are more powerful than the later ones. All the legal and moral relations of society developed from the institutions of *property*, which is the primary element in economy. It was only on the basis of property that *agriculture*, the strongest and surest basis for all the higher forms of society in all ages, could develop. And on the basis of agriculture *commerce* developed, which in turn brought about the use of *money*, one of the most powerful media of higher interaction, civilization, and progress, as well as all the other means of human communication.

Likewise, the primary form of human organization, the family, remained through all times the basis of all later, higher forms of association—of tribes, nations and states.

Since the earlier is more independent and more powerful than the later, the earlier a thing develops the more absolute it is, and the later it develops the more relative it is.

CHAPTER VII

*Since the earlier things are more powerful, they
receive and spend larger quantities of the available, limited, general energy, while the later ones
receive less, and are thereby weaker.*

Since the greatest part of the energy of nature was
spent in the creation of the inorganic world, and a
large part of the remainder for the development of
the organic, there remains very little for man and for
the development of his civilization. And as mankind
lives only on the surplus of the energy of the earth's
life, so man's psychic life persists only on the surplus
of his energy, of his physical life. Man is a luxury of
nature, thinking is a luxury of man.

Not only individual men but peoples as well spend
the greatest part of their energy for their physical
maintenance; the needs of physical life consume the
greatest part of man's nervous energy. All the other,
higher functions of the brain—observation, thinking,
and so on—are merely its secondary and superfluous
activities, and are very little developed in most men,
since they depend on the least quantity of nervous
energy, the left-over from the prior processes.

In the same way every people spends the largest
part of its energy for the preservation of its physical,
sensual life. Therefore, only those peoples rise to the
level of history, only those have value for the progress
of mankind, to which there remains a surplus of

energy for higher, historical life. The peoples who have to spend all their efforts for their mere preservation do not have value for mankind and its history and progress. In all times the production of goods necessary to the preservation of physical life has absorbed the greatest part of social energy; there are very few peoples in history that have been able to contribute and that are contributing to progress.

Since art has always absorbed much more of the excess of human energy which remains unspent in the struggle for existence than have sciences and philosophy, the abstract thought, among all peoples, has always subsisted only on the meager surplus. And of all the arts, it is architecture, among all peoples, which has absorbed most of this excess.

CHAPTER VIII

Since all that which is earlier receives more of the available general energy, and since it has fewer requirements and conditions for its existence and preservation, the earlier things develop and maintain themselves more easily than the later, with less need for struggle and exertion. Accordingly, later things, receiving less of the general energy, and having, the later they appear, ever more increasing difficulties, maintain themselves under ever greater hardships, and must struggle more and more painfully for their preservation; the later things are weaker than the earlier, and perish the more easily the later they come into being.

1. As the more highly developed forms of life have more difficulties in maintaining themselves, perishing the more readily because of the increasing number of enemies and obstacles, life is, in general, a luxury of the earth, subsisting only on that part of her energy which is available for luxury.

The latest living phenomenon, man, is the weakest of all; he develops with the most hardship and maintains himself most painfully, his existence requires the most effort, the bitterest struggles; he has the most numerous natural enemies and is least protected by nature. The struggle with nature is much sharper, much more difficult for man than for the animals, and since he receives nothing ready-made from nature, he has to acquire his learning laboriously. Animals, on the other hand, bring to the world almost ready-made the equipment they need for meeting the problems of their existence. Man is the least satisfied of all the animals on the earth, because he has more needs than any other, and can scarcely satisfy them all. And considering man as such, primitive, natural man maintains himself much more easily, and much less painfully than the later, higher, historical man. The primitive man has only the lower, physical needs and satisfies them more easily, for things which can satisfy man's primary, important needs are much more abundant, accessible and easily obtainable than things that satisfy his later, higher needs. The lower the man (on the evolutionary and historical scale), the more nature itself takes care of him, the more easily he maintains himself. With every progressive step man is left more and more to himself. Without any external help or stimulus from nature, he becomes more and more directed upon his fellow human beings; thereby man becomes increasingly necessary and indispensable to man: One consequence of this process is what we call humaneness. Higher, historical man must satisfy his higher needs by himself. He has to seek out, acquire and maintain all the later, historical goods by himself. His civilization is maintained only by an unnatural strain on his energy. All historical acquisitions are destroyed by natural forces, whenever and wherever they are not carefully tended by man. Since in all times the largest quantities of human energy have been spent in acquiring food, and since all progress increasingly tends to facilitate the providing of food for more and more people, it follows that at all times the smallest part of man's energy has been available for the preservation of civilization, his most precious historical acquisition. As nature maintains him, so does man preserve his culture only with the surplus of his strength; hence the civilizations of various peoples and epochs have always been preserved with the greatest difficulties, and have always perished most easily.

Since only the higher, historical man improves civilization and advances reason, since only he acquires those sublime, noble and precious historical goods of man, and not the lower man, the man of the genus, it follows that the higher the man, the higher the goods for which he struggles, the more painful he finds it to acquire and maintain what he needs. The lower the man, on the other hand, the less pain he feels; his pains in themselves are lower and consequently not so lasting, his requirements may be satisfied more easily than those of the higher man. The lower, sensual man finds himself quickly in life. He goes along his way more easily, satisfies his lower, sensual needs with less difficulty; the goal he has to reach is closer, the height he desires to surmount is lower, he is easily saturated with what nature and his society give him, and does not look for anything else. For the higher, nobler individual, with his deeper soul and finer spirit, there is nothing ready-made in the world; he must stumble and struggle for a long time; in his path there are many obstacles, and because he frequently fails to reach his individual goals, his pains are deeper and more enduring than those of the lower man.

Since one comes to the highest and most valuable good—spirit and consciousness—only by a very painful development, and since consciousness is maintained and stimulated only by pain, it follows that the higher the level of consciousness, the greater the intensity of pain and sorrow.

The brain, as the weakest organ, tires the most easily and needs the most rest and compensation, while the lower organs need less rest. Accordingly, thinking is the most strenuous human activity, and is carried on with more difficulty than the functioning of the other organs, and is more easily disturbed than the other functions. Mental exertion is more strenuous than physical labor and spends much more of the total determined energy allotted to the individual, and, accordingly, manual labor is easier, and to the average person more pleasant than intellectual effort.

Likewise, all that is unconscious, all that must be, appears and maintains itself without strain and painful effort; all the instinctive activities of man occur by themselves, spontaneously; man does not have to study or practice them to become skilled; they occur independently of his will and conscious endeavor.

Thinking is also more difficult than feeling, consumes much more of the general quantity of blood and energy, and maintains itself with more difficulty than feeling; hence it is much easier to write emotionally than intellectually. Since a large majority of people live a purely emotional life, it is easier to write for them than for the minority of rationally minded persons. Thus poets and artists who create largely emotional works, and whose appeal is largely directed to the emotions are closer to the majority of people and better understood by them than are philosophers and scientists who work for the intellect.

Likewise, in the realm of spirit, the prior appears and maintains itself more easily than the posterior. Imagination appears spontaneously and does not require any effort or study from man, while for conscious thinking, for the process which leads to truth, to be maintained, he must continually study and exert himself. Accordingly, truth stands toward man in the same way man stands toward nature and the things of nature: As man maintains himself in nature only with great difficulty, pain and struggle, so does truth among men. There remains, to a very small number of individuals, some surplus of energy from the struggle for living to undertake the even more painful and difficult struggle for truth, for knowledge cannot be inhaled like air, nor can it be acquired as easily as food and water; it is gained only laboriously. So the large majority of people soon reach the limits of their power of thinking; their knowledge remains at that level which is necessary for present life and society. Only a few human beings rise to the height of science and philosophy, and still fewer of them contribute to the progress of thought.

The primary knowledge which one secures through the senses is far more directly obtained and easily maintained than the later, higher knowledge, which is acquired by means of abstract thinking, and preserved in the awakened consciousness. And because sensual knowledge is easier to gain than abstract understanding, induction is easier than deduction, sensual observation is easier than thinking, knowledge is easier than understanding. So practice is easier than theory; it is easier to find one's way in everyday life than in the sphere of ideas, and, likewise, it is easier to live in the present than to work on the development of ideas. Even sense knowledge acquired in childhood and youth leaves much stronger and more lasting effects than knowledge acquired later, for later in life there is less energy available for preserving new impressions. Thus, while feelings and perceptions recently acquired disappear rapidly, earlier perceptions and impressions persist.

It is easier to work successfully in the fields of natural sciences, whose subjects are accessible to the senses, than it is to work in the humanities; this is why the natural sciences developed before the studies of man.

As the earlier, sense knowledge is more easily acquired than the later abstract forms, and as one can, through sense perception, know only individual parts and not wholes, it is always easier to recognize parts than it is to recognize wholes. It is much easier to grasp individual forces, things, phenomena and aspects than to understand their common connections, their unified activities. Hence philosophy is the most difficult task of the human spirit, for it requires more work and exertion than anything else; the greatest undertaking of the human mind is to attempt to rise to the height of principle, from which one can see a single great whole in which all phenomena are merely various manifestations of one and the same original force, in which all things and elements are simply particular vibrations of one fundamental tone. This is why only a few mighty intellects can rise to the height of principle, and even they only after long and strenuous effort, after study and thought.

Because the sensual is much closer and much more readily accessible to the lower minds of the majority of human beings, the more sensual the things are, the more readily maintained they are in life, the more easily they strike root, while the higher and later, the more abstract and noble ones, do so with ever greater difficulty. Humaneness and social consciousness establish and maintain themselves with much more difficulty than egoism and selfishness. The lower man feels and understands the community, the people, the state and mankind much less easily than he does his family and his selfish personal interests.

As only the surface of things can be perceived through the senses, and as truth is always found in the depths and must be searched for strenuously, the error is always found, accepted and maintained much more easily than the truth. The error strikes root in man's mind much more easily and deeply than the truth; only error lifts man and flatters him about his greatness, power and value, while every great and profound truth limits the value, greatness and power of man, and lowers him more and more to a will-less, impotent thing in the general process of being. So the cold, indifferent truth is maintained with difficulty, while the warm and friendly error is easily preserved.

Accordingly, artistic activity is easier than intellectual, and art can maintain itself more easily than science and philosophy, for art satisfies a need for the large majority of people, and has fewer powerful enemies and obstacles to overcome than science and philosophy. Truth and reason have always had to fight the greatest number of obstacles and enemies; they have always been bought with the greatest sacrifices, and are therefore the most difficult to preserve of all human things. In all times of great social stress philosophy and science are the first things to disappear, for their life depends upon the greatest number of favorable conditions.

Religion, the belief in the power of nature over man, appears and endures a great deal more easily than do later philosophy and science. It touches the most primitive parts of man's nature, the feelings of joy and sorrow, hope and desire, and since it is more easily preserved, it perishes with more difficulty than

do science and philosophy with their laws and principles. For religious belief man need not think or suffer
strain; religion grows spontaneously from the human
soul, while science, a more subtle thing, requires
permanent cultivation and protection from external
dangers. Yet the later, higher and nobler forms of
religion are maintained with greater difficulty and
perish more easily than earlier, lower ones. The
primitive belief in fetishes, in good and evil spirits, in
the continuous intervention of God in human affairs,
is rooted far more deeply in the human mind, and
thus appears and maintains itself much more readily
than the later, higher belief in a remote God who
directs all things according to reason and law; for the
majority of ordinary people the idea of one God is too
high and abstract a notion to be recognized in the
multitude of different things and phenomena. The
masses will always be satisfied with the lower forms of
religion; their minds will always reside at the primitive levels of faith. Thus Christianity, with its belief in
one righteous God and its preaching of love and
brotherhood, has been able, throughout its long existence, to root itself only shallowly in the ordinary
human soul; it has created only a thin stratum in it,
which life and lower forms of faith break and spoil at
every step.

Just as historical, humane man maintains himself
with much more difficulty, with many more struggles
and a great deal more anguish than the natural man,
so do the higher forms of human society have a more
difficult struggle to subsist than the primitive ones—
tribes and families. Every human community is composed of a majority who work only for themselves and
their narrow personal goals, and a minority who sac-
rifice themselves in working for the common goods of

185

society and fighting the common evils and dangers. If society is to maintain itself, the social virtues are needed; but these are delicate flowers, while selfishness grows and develops with the ease of weeds. Justice and morality, these late and tender acquisitions of man, are the very weak obstacles which modern society opposes to the natural selfishness of man. This is why they are frequently trampled under foot, and why selfishness is confined to the prescribed and allowable limits only through strenuous efforts. Most people can be compelled to fulfill their social duties and obligations only by force and necessity, authority and religion.

Man must suppress much of his animal nature in order to live in society and to preserve it; and as he must blunt his senses in order to permit reason to develop, so must he stupefy his animal instincts in order to make room within himself for the humane, social man.

Thus peoples and states, the later, higher forms through which mankind passes in the course of history, are preserved with much more difficulty than the earlier ones—tribes and families; there is no state in history that has not suffered from many shocks and revolutions from without and from within; there is no people that has not shed rivers of blood and made many other sacrifices in order to maintain itself.

As it is only the higher strata of society that carry civilization and progress, civilization is preserved only with difficulty, and readily disappears in periods of stress, both internal and external. In major respects mankind has made very little real progress, and what has been made is being maintained with great difficulty and has been paid for very dearly, in struggle and effort.

Thus the beautiful and noble is acquired only at the price of great pains and sacrifices; the greater the good, the more difficult is it to acquire and to preserve. All civilization, all man's progress in the beautiful, good and true, is acquired and maintained with blood and hardships; they are never happened upon or given as gifts. Thus it is that all the evils, pains and sorrows of the higher man result from the consciousness of his weakness, from his knowledge of the difficulty of preserving his expensively created noble and beautiful acquisitions, from the difficulty of reaching justice and truth. Thus the later is ever more unnecessary, ever more a luxury, and is preserved with ever greater strain.

2. Since the earlier is more easily preserved, it is more easily inherited; *the earlier a trait appears, the more likely it is to enter the common heritage, the later, the less.*

The earlier things lie deeper in the organism, have deeper roots in soul and body and, accordingly, are more easily inherited and preserved. The later things have less room, strike shallower roots, are closer to the surface, can be more easily disturbed and destroyed, and are, thus, less likely to be inherited. Instincts are the most easily transmitted by heredity; both animals and man inherit instincts of self-preservation and of reproduction. So feelings, sense abilities, moral and immoral inclinations and impulses, and physical traits and powers are inherited more readily than later elements of the psyche and spirit. Intellectual capabilities are the rarest and most difficult to inherit, and, consequently, are more difficult to preserve than the lower, prior elements of the mind. Intellect, the most recent faculty of man, was acquired by purely human effort, and has never been the heritage of the human species. Intellectual ability is a superficial, feeble characteristic that cannot impress any lasting traces in the organism, to be carried over to the offspring with the more basic psychic forces. Spirit and intellect are the acquisitions of a few exalted individuals, and can be inherited only through history.

3. As the earlier is more easily preserved than the later, *the earlier the thing, the more enduring it is; the later it is, the more perishable.*

CHAPTER IX

As later things perish and die easily and rapidly, and maintain themselves with ever greater difficulties, the later a thing, the shorter its existence, while the earlier it occurs, the more enduring it is. The durability of things is proportional to their priority in time.

1. The laws of nature—mechanical, physical, chemical and physiological—embrace man throughout his lifetime, while the laws of society and history, the laws of community and of spirit, begin to affect him in only a few aspects, as he matures. The social and historical personality is only a passing moment in man's life, while the natural man lives from birth to death. Similarly, consciousness, the highest point in the mind's development, where the psyche rests for the shortest time, is only a passing moment in human life, while the primitive, the unconscious, lasts throughout. Consciousness occupies the shortest period in the life of all people.

And in the human psyche as well, those natural, primitive traits and forces, which in their rudiments man brings into the world with his body, are much more enduring than those that are acquired later, through education and experience—the results of time and society—the results of history. Man sooner stops thinking than feeling; reason lasts only for a short part of the lifetime of an individual and of a people. Thus the psyche always retains the ability to experience the primary emotions, especially that of fear (which must be retained for the sake of self-preservation), but the capacity for the later, higher affections—love, joy and sorrow—is not so enduring, and ceases earlier than the capacity for the more elementary affections. Love passes in the same way as consciousness and free will; it is the peak from which one soon descends to a more lasting phase of life— that of indifference. Consciousness, the highest level man can reach, and on which he remains for the briefest period, is only a passing moment in the general process of his life; the primitive and instinctive remains even when consciousness has gone; the animal and vegetative survive all human aspects. And just as one passes much more quickly from consciousness into unconsciousness than in the reverse direction, as the period of life itself fills in the earth's history the briefest interval of her existence, the proportion between the conscious and unconscious life is the same in every individual and in every people.

In all societies, and in all mankind, the age of philosophy and science lasts for the shortest period of time, while religion accompanies man from the cradle to the grave; it survives philosophy and the sciences, which latter are only a passing phase in the history of the human mind. Similarly, man is older than tribe and people, which are only individual forms of mankind, and when the life of tribes and peoples exhausts itself, there will remain only man, who will survive all his historical manifestations.

If the world's life were a clock, man's life, throughout his whole history, would last only a second, organic life a minute and the inorganic life of matter the whole length of time. The entire life of mankind, from the beginning to the end, is the briefest period of the earth's existence; it is the most fragile thread in the complexity of her life, and will be broken in the slightest strain.

2. *Since the prior is more lasting and necessary than the posterior, the earlier a thing, the more enduring is the need for it, and, likewise, the later it occurs, the more transitory is the need it satisfies.*

The sun, with its light and warmth, air, water, vegetation, have been necessities for man in all times, and he will need these as long as he himself exists. The need for fire, tools, writing, and agriculture continues the same in all epochs of history, while the press, railway and telegraph, for instance, were needed only in certain later times.

Accordingly, the value and significance of the earlier things are more lasting than those of the later ones which have a more passing importance.

3. *Since the earlier is more lasting than the later, the dependence of later things upon the earlier ones is also more enduring. The earlier a thing, the more enduring a condition of later things it represents.*

Today civilization no longer depends on external nature, on favorable locations in convenient regions of the earth, as it did in its first phases, just as man's opinions and ideas no longer rest on external nature and on its impressions in the human mind. All religious ideas, and even the theory of geocentrics, result from the influence of external nature on the mind of man. Man's intellect, as well as the progress of civilization, depend increasingly on the earlier, deeper forces, those which are prior to external nature, those which were active before nature received its present external shape. The higher the reason, the more vigorously it emancipates itself from the dependence on later developments—body and society, present events, and external nature.

Man can never free himself from the influence of the sun and the basic inorganic forces and phenomena, while he is progressively freeing himself from the influence of later developments—animals, plants, soil and climate.

CHAPTER X

Since the earlier is more lasting than the later,
it occupies more of the limited general time avail-
able to the whole of life; the longer a thing lasts,
the more slowly it comes into being. Accordingly,
the earlier a thing appears, the more of that lim-
ited whole of time it occupies, the later, the less.
Consequently, the earlier a thing, the more slowly
it develops and the more slowly it disappears.

However great were the number of years spent in
the development of the earth's strata and in the form-
ing of her present shape, the proportion between the
prior and the posterior moments of her life remains
the same: The first phase is the longest, and the succeeding ones are shorter and shorter; man, the last
phase, is the shortest of all. And the primitive period
of man's existence occupies the greatest part of his
total allotted time. Man consumed the longest period
of his life for the preparation of the physical basis for
his later spiritual advancement. The later period, beginning with the discovery of fire and tools, the development of language, and the first societies, and the
last one, beginning with the first states and lasting to
the present, occupy the shortest part of man's life on
earth.

Thus, the first discoveries and inventions took man many thousands of years, while the great majority of later discoveries and inventions are concentrated in the short interval of a few centuries. Similarly, the prehistoric evolution of language occupied a much longer span of time than its historical developments.

CHAPTER XI

Since the earlier lasts longer than the later, its influence is more continuous than that of the later; the later a thing, the more subject its activity is to interruption.

As the vegetative elements in the organism act more continuously than the animal elements, so the earlier, physiological forces are more constant than the later, psychic ones: The earlier a thing, the more likely it is to be carried over and preserved by heredity. Breathing begins at the first moment and does not stop throughout life, persisting through all the conscious and unconscious phases and through all changes and crises.

Likewise, every man is a permanent and continuous subject-matter of chemistry, biology and zoology; for he is continually subjected to their laws, while only individual men, races, classes and epochs rise to become the subjects of history, whose laws, woven from the thinnest and weakest threads, are the most easily and frequently broken and transgressed.

As the earlier is more necessary and lasting, it is, likewise, a more constant need, while the later is the necessity of only particular moments. As the press, science and civilization are the needs of only particular epochs and particular men, so mankind as a whole, with all its history and civilization, is the need of only a moment in the life of the earth.

CHAPTER XII

The earlier a thing is, the more powerfully it influences all later things which depend upon it: In order to appear and maintain itself, the posterior must draw on the prior for energy and nourishment.

As plants and animals derive their food primarily from the prior, inorganic forces and materials, so the intellect absorbs its food and energy only from the prior emotions. For the intellectual to have any social effect, it must be strengthened and supported by feeling. Religious ideas, affecting man's feelings, his pleasures and pains, strike root, expand, grow stronger and act in society much more rapidly than purely intellectual ones. The only strong and efficient ideas are those awakened, strengthened and stimulated by the emotions; only the feeling of truth gives strength to truth. Since the feeling of benefit is one of the strongest moving forces of mankind, all the great social ideas are nothing else than formulas of the interests of millions of people. The greater the idea, the greater is the number of people whose problems it solves.

Thus, science and philosophy get their nourishment from religion; the deeper and higher the religion, the more profound are the philosophical and scientific concepts and theories which evolve from it. Religion clears the way for science and philosophy and supplies them with the first stimuli in the fight against other, inferior forces. The appearance of new religions and religious revolutions and reforms always have refreshed the human mind, given it new energy, and prepared it for new adventures, efforts and successes.

Impulses and feelings, longings and strivings, hopes and anticipations of the masses strengthen, stimulate and lead noble and elevated minds in their thinking and activity. The higher social and historical life of man rises upon the feelings, strivings and hopes of the masses. As the human laws derive their life and strength from customs, so the laws promulgated by great and noble minds are effective only if they result from the wishes and tendencies of the common man, only if they absorb and radiate the hopes and aspirations of the people.

Since everything later nourishes and strengthens itself at the expense of the earlier, the later a thing occurs, the more consumptive it is; the earlier it occurs, the more productive it is. And as all the later things are strengthened and nourished by earlier ones, all later things exist and develop only at the expense of the earlier.

Later things become strong only as earlier ones become weak. The decreased intensity of the cosmic aspects of general development brought about an increase in the biological; similarly, the reason is sharpened at the expense of the senses; the keenness of the higher senses depends upon the blunting of the lower ones (smell and touch are sharper among the deaf and the blind). Likewise, civilization, humaneness and generosity develop only at the expense of the animal in man; man must lose much of his animal freshness and warmth in order to be able to live in society. Reason, which consumes more energy than any other activity, develops at the expense of the energy of all the prior processes.

Since all the posterior develops and grows stronger only at the expense of the prior, the later a thing, the more destructive it is of the prior things; the earlier a thing, the more constructive it is. Accordingly, the earlier things are, the more constructive they are for the later ones; the later they are, the less creative they are.

Just as in the first phases of the earth's development her creative energy was greater in the creation and destruction of inorganic and organic forms than it is today, so were the first periods of man's history much more creative than the later ones; at the time of historical beginnings all the main foundations upon which all later developments rest were laid down; all the principal types, forms and characteristics of the whole later development of mankind were created. Later historical epochs only develop, only elaborate the things created in those first times, only continue to weave the threads spun from the natural, animal life.

Since earlier things are more creative, and since all the later ones depend upon the earlier, it follows that first things are more original and more typical of all that follows than are things which develop later. As the earth's position with regard to the sun gives type to all earthly things, from inorganic forms to the ideas of man, so the first ideas that man formed about himself and about the world gave type to all his later thinking.

CHAPTER XIII

Since all the earlier is the necessary condition of all the later, all the prior is an ingredient of the posterior. Thus, all later things are composed of all earlier ones, and accordingly, contain more and more elements, while the earlier things are less complex. The complexity of things is proportional to their posteriority in time.

The latest being on earth, man, is composed of all the prior, inorganic and organic forces, elements and characteristics. And as the successive elements of nature become permanent elements of man's organism, so do the successive periods of human history become elements of civilization at later levels of historical development; primitive man settles into the masses of historical society. As biology is subject to the laws of mathematics, mechanics, astronomy, geology, physics and chemistry, so is the life of civilized man subject to these same laws and to those of physiology, psychology, sociology and history as well.

The later the period of history, the more elements, human and natural, from previous times it contains; the later the life of mankind, the more numerous and the more interlaced are the threads of which civilization and the historical life of man are woven, the more numerous and the more complicated are the factors, forces and phenomena of civilization. Thus, also a great truth or a profound idea is composed of facts and laws, of beliefs, knowledge and understanding, of the beautiful, the good, the righteous and the necessary, of feelings, pains and pleasures and of the thinking of men of all earlier times. Every real truth must be at the same time beautiful, good and necessary. Truth illuminates from its heights the good and beautiful, the righteous and necessary, and upon truth's warmth and light depends the quantity of goodness, beauty and justice in the world.

Consequently, the earlier a science, the simpler is the subject-matter with which it is concerned. The last science—the history of mankind—embraces all inorganic and organic, social and psychic, forces and laws; all religions, philosophies, arts and sciences; all races, tribes, peoples, states and personalities; all discoveries, events, wars and struggles. History is an organized complex of all human sentiments, thoughts, souls, spirits and times. In order to understand the life of man from the perspective of history, one must comprehend all the forces that influenced mankind in all times. To unsnarl only one thread of man's history one must descend through the depths of the strata of the whole history of mankind, to the general processes of the organic and the inorganic; to understand one present phenomenon one must know the entire past. Since the history of mankind is the last and most complicated result of all the vital forces of nature, in order to understand the history of man one must know the entire history of nature.

Accordingly, history stands toward all other sciences as a whole organism toward its parts. All peoples and states, all religions, literatures and philosophies, all sciences and epochs are only the individual parts, organs, forces and episodes of that one great whole—universal history.

CHAPTER XIV

*Since the earlier is ever less complex, the later
ever more so, it follows that the earlier the things
are, the more equal and uniform they are; the
later they are, the more diverse and differentiated.*

The primary physical aspects of life are the same
for all human beings: Physically mankind forms but
one species; among the people of the various races
and tribes there are no essential differences. The
number of teeth, fingers, bones and senses is the same
in all races; all men walk erect and speak; there is no
natural difference in life expectancy and length of
pregnancy; all people have approximately the same
quantity of blood, and it circulates at approximately
the same temperature in all of them. And on the first,
natural level of humanness all human beings are
equal, just as the products and tools of primitive man
are equal in all times and places.

And as primitive man settles into the masses of the
later historical societies, the masses of all historical
epochs are equal in their feelings and ideas, needs
and aspirations; there is no difference among them
either in times or in peoples. Thus, it is only the lower
men, who form the masses of societies and of peoples,
who are equal among themselves. And also, all men in
general, both lower and higher, are equal in their
primitive, lower, bodily needs, as they are the same at
the beginnings of their individual lives, as in childhood all languages are also the same. So everyone is
equal in his basic natural needs and capacities; the

differences arise in the mind and spirit. Natural, biological man is everywhere equal; there is, however, more difference in morality among men, especially among those of reason; there is only one biological species of man, but there are several species of psyches.

Primitive language—the language of bodily movements and of interjections—is the same in all men and at all times. The facial expressions in joy and in sorrow are the same in all races, just as wonder and fear are also manifested everywhere in the same way. Only later, spoken languages differ with different peoples.

CHAPTER XV

Since everything later is composed of the earlier—as earlier things are the elements of later ones—the earlier becomes common to ever larger numbers of occurrences, while the later and later is less and less common.

Reproduction, nutrition, growth and death are the most general aspects of living, common to plants and animals in the same way as is the idea of organism. Sensibility is likewise a characteristic common to every animal: All animals, including man, feel.

The primary natural needs for food, shelter and copulation are the first, common stimuli of movements and activities among animals and among most of mankind. Later, higher stimuli, which appear at the higher levels of man's historical development as a result of higher needs, are limited to later, and increasingly restricted circles of higher human beings. Hence, work which is independent of lower kinds of stimuli, of body, life and present is limited to the smallest circle of higher, historical men.

The earlier the phases of life, the more common they are to an ever greater number of men; the later they are, the more restricted they are to ever smaller circles. The entire human species passes through the phase of primitive, natural, non-historical life; the tribe, as a social form, is common to all barbarians, peoples who grew out of the natural stage, but who have not yet entered history. Only certain particular tribes rise to the levels of states and nations; the ideas of state and nation arise later and are too high for the large majority of lower men, while the idea of one mankind and of man's common interests are restricted to only a few individual minds.

Not only are things, forces and characteristics more common according to their priority in time, but also, the earlier they are, the more generally needed they are by ever larger numbers of things. As air is a need common to all organic beings, so is the family necessary to all human beings, and architecture to all the arts. Religion is a need common to all people in all times. And its primitive phases, fetishism and polytheism, are more commonly needed, by more men and in more different times, than monotheism, the highest form of religion, which is needed by only a few higher individuals in each epoch.

CHAPTER XVI

Since all later things are composed of earlier ones, all the later, uniting within itself all the earlier, reconciles the contradictions of the earlier.

Modern geology reconciles vulcanism and neptunism, maintaining that both catastrophes and peaceful evolution are only individual phases of the general process of development. Likewise, modern biology reconciles the opposed ideas of creation and of evolution, giving the opposed principles of heredity and adaptation their proper place in the process of life, reconciling conservative and progressive, the theory of revolution with that of evolution. Likewise, modern psychology reconciles sensualism with idealism. In the same way, having established the principles of movement and living of mankind in all times and places, scientific history will reconcile within itself all the contrasts which have successively arisen in it—contrasts between man and nature, spirit and matter, senses and intellect, feeling, belief and knowledge, individual and society, ideal and real.

As the higher and higher civilization increasingly embraces and reconciles within itself all the historical elements which have successively appeared, and each of which, appearing, entered the struggle against all the others; as the modern state, uniting within itself, more and more reconciles all social and historical elements, giving each its proper place in the general social structure—so does modern society endeavor more and more to reconcile all opposed historical and social forces and elements, personal and common interests, individual and society, and thereby to harmonize interests and ideas, justice and truth, with life and usefulness, with the interests of existence; in other words, to reconcile the will and interests of individuals with general laws, the individuality of persons with the whole social organization; to harmonize order with progress and freedom with justice.

CHAPTER XVII

Since all the earlier is needed by all the later, by
an ever increasing number of things, since the
earlier is, in other words, more generally
needed—because it is common to all the later—it
follows that the earlier a thing is, the more there is
of it, the more generally distributed it is, and,
accordingly, the later it is, the less there is of it.
The general distribution of things is proportional
to their priority in time.

The inorganic, as earlier than the organic, is more
general than the organic, which represents only a
small part of the inorganic. There are very few places
in the universe in which organic life can awake from
the inorganic and maintain itself; and even on the
earth, the quantity of inorganic matter is vastly greater than that of the entire organic world. Aside from
the fact that the inorganic in nature far outweighs the
organic, in the organic realm itself the inorganic is the
preponderant element. In the human body, just as in
all other organisms, water is the most general and the
most stable ingredient.

Likewise, the laws of the inorganic world are more
general than those of the organic, and stand toward
the latter in the same proportion as the inorganic
stands toward the organic.

In the inorganic realm itself, the general distribution of particular inorganic forces is proportional to their priority in time.

Heat is the most general of all the organic and inorganic forces, in all space and time; it is a general factor of all creation and being, from cosmic worlds to the birth of man and of human thought, just as the sense of warmth is more general than any other sense. So also the laws of mechanical processes are more general than the physical and chemical ones. Light is less general than warmth; it is limited to a much smaller part of space than heat is; there is much more of the dark, unillumed and invisible, than there is of the illumed and visible, and even the sense of warmth is, like warmth itself, more generally distributed than the sense of light. Of all the senses only the eye is sensitive to light (while all the body is sensitive to warmth). In the same way there is much more darkness than light even in man's psyche, and likewise there is far less of what can be seen by the eye of sense, i.e., illuminated objects, than there is of unilluminated, dark and hidden ones. In every individual, moreover, there is a greater amount of what is obscure and hidden than there is of that part of his essence which can be observed, or which is or can be expressed; much more of the inexpressible than of the expressible. Again, man is able to see very little of the Whole, but he is still less able to *foresee!*

Since only the surface of things is illuminated, there is much more of the internal than of the external; *the earlier a thing is, the more inward it is, the less externalized.* There is far more of that which man cannot express, which he has never expressed or will be able to express, than there is of that which he is able to. There are many, many phenomena in the world, but very few words capable of describing them. And just as the number of expressions is so much smaller than the number of things, so in every human society only a few individuals define the plans and aspirations; only a few speak in the name of all; only a few clearly express the wishes and hopes of an entire society or an entire epoch; the majority of every society is a mute, expressionless mass.

Since primitive, natural man gravitates into the masses of historical society, the mass-man has all the characteristics and abilities of the primitive. He sees and apprehends only what is accessible to the senses and, accordingly, sees and conceives only the real and material, never rising to the abstract. Accordingly, he does not perceive the process, but sees and appreciates only the result. Observing only real facts and examples, he understands only the particular, and not the general. As a consequence, the mass-man sees and lives only in the present. He sees only the surface, only the visible and audible; he is aware only of personalities. Subjected to the senses in everything, even in love, the primitive is sensual even in his morality; the morality of the majority is determined only by their longings and interests, their selfishness and vanity, passions, cupidities and fears. Such lower emotions and needs are the stimuli to activity for a large majority of human beings. Similarly, the mass-man is sensual also in his religion. Seeing in activity only persons, he can be led only by persons, he obeys only individuals. As the mass is led only by personalities, every idea must be incarnated in great individualities before it can master the masses. Hence, the mass-man only imitates—he is capable only of imitation. This is why there is so little of the original, individual and independent in everything human; this is why the great majority rises only to physical individuality, why spiritually they always remain dependent upon the minority of higher, original and independent human beings, those who create new forms, clear new ways, and discover new laws and ideas. There is indeed little of the individual in every human society, little of the original, the independent, the creative, and much more of the elemental, the reproductive and the imitative.

Since the consciousness of lesser man is directed primarily toward the external, present and real, he never rises above the practical and useful. Hence the majority of intellectual creations are craftsmanly, practical; moreover, for the majority, not only work but morality itself consists only of practical activities. All this is natural, for practical abilities are much more widespread in mankind than the theoretical ones; thus, there is a great deal more of knowledge than of understanding, of things and facts than of laws and ideas.

Since (Chap. 24)* things settle and become fixed one above the other in the determined and limited general space in the same order in which they separate from the great, primordial, universal whole, it follows that the earlier a thing is, the deeper it lies, the more space it occupies, the more generalized it is. And, accordingly, the later a thing appears, the less room it has, the higher it has to climb, the less general it is, and the more constricted. Since from the single great primordial whole of the human species, *natural, savage man* was the first to separate, he occupied the largest part of the limited space of human history, he lies at its deepest level and most of it is concerned with him. Much time passed before there separated from

* *Part Two*

210

the whole of the human species smaller and smaller groups of *ever more social, humane, historical man,* for whom there remains less and less place, whose number is ever smaller, but who mounts to ever greater heights. Accordingly, in every society there is much more of the natural, primitive man than there is of the historical, humane.

So in every human society the mass of natural, primitive, lesser men always constitute the large majority, and all the energy, all the higher forces of mankind are concentrated in and expressed by only a small number of higher, noble individuals.

The primary need for *food* is the most general need of all human beings in every society. The search for food is the primary and therefore most common stimulus to work for everyone. In the first historical times, as well as in the beginning of each individual life, man spends his time and energy only for the provision of food and the maintenance of bodily life. This primal necessity remains in all historical epochs the most general need for every man and every society. This is why food products are the most necessary and general products in every country, and why the acquisition of food consumes the greatest amount of value produced by each person. Likewise, the life of a large majority of people in every society does not rise above the satisfaction of the stomach and other bodily needs. The production of food engages the largest part of the social effort and in every society the procurement of food engages the largest stratum of population.

As the majority of human beings consume the greatest part of their labor, energy and time for securing food and maintaining their physical life, there remains, in all societies, a very small surplus of the total energy to be expended in progress. This is why the progress of mankind is so scant and slow. There are only a very few people in each age in which that surplus energy of mankind is concentrated, that left-over unspent for the maintenance of the body, and these are the ones who discover new truths, invent new things and clear new paths.

As food is a natural, primal need of man, so is *feeling* a natural, primary activity: Thus, it is more general than the later, historical abilities, such as thinking and reason. All animals and all men feel, but only man, or better, only a few human beings, think. Hence, the majority of activities of most people result from the emotions—from fear, hope, profit, love, hatred—and very rarely from the later, higher notion of the *should,* of duty. Accordingly, all morality in society is limited to a small number of people, since among the greater part of mankind natural stimuli prevail—emotions, bodily impulses and sensual urges; the activities of most people have therefore no moral value; the majority of every society is from a moral standpoint weak and poorly developed.

Even the sense organization of the body is better developed than its intellectual one. The parts of the brain that mediate sensation constitute the largest part of its mass, while the parts that condition reasoning occupy a smaller share. Accordingly, in every man there is much more feeling than thinking, and in every society the people who think are much fewer than those who just feel. Reason is the scantest and weakest of all human attributes.

Likewise, language is far more expressive of emotion than of reason; the language of feelings is the most universal language of mankind. The most primitive language, expressing only emotional actions—interjections—is common to all men and even to the animals.

And all great religions (which are the only theories and philosophies of the masses) preoccupy themselves more with emotions than they do with thoughts, and affect the feelings more than the reason. The multitudes are never led by reason, but by emotions, desires and passions; accordingly, every truth intended to penetrate the masses, and which ought to reach them, should be bound up with feelings: It should affect the emotions, in order that the masses may be able to accept it. Since a large majority of people feel more than they think, the majority will always be moved by and interested in that which affects emotions more than by that which affects the reason. Hence, poets, artists and religious reformers who play on sentiment always influence more people and are better known than men who appeal to the intellect. This is why in every literature there is much more of poetry than of science and philosophy, since, as it was said before, it is easier to write for the emotions than for the reason, as feeling, in general, is much easier than thinking.

Just as nature is much larger than man in it, so in man himself there is much more of the natural than on the humane and historical. As only a very small part of inorganic matter develops into organic life, so only a very small part of the organic evolves into man: Among the things in nature, *man* is the scarcest of all. So also in every man there is much more of the primitive, natural forces of the mind than of the later, historically acquired ones. And just as man has many more relations with nature, with the soil, with plants and animals, than with other human beings, so also the majority of the sciences, arts and crafts result

213

from man's relations with matter; nature provides many more objects and fields for human activity than does man with his affairs.

Likewise, every man is much more subject to the natural sciences—mechanics, physics, chemistry, biology and physiology—than he is to psychology and history. Only a few, higher men rise to become subject to history, while the majority stay out of history, and without history, neither acting upon it nor participating in it, living only the life of nature. Accordingly, although man is the most individualized natural creation, even the large majority of *his* kind rise only to physical individuality, so that, in general, men are merely exemplars of a type.

The history of mankind, the process of its life, its progress and civilization may be compared to a long highway, broad at the beginning, and progressively narrowing into the distance. All mankind passed through the primitive, animal, natural phase of life, and every individual man does likewise, but only particular races and particular nations pass through the higher levels, and to the most advanced phases only the rare spirits attain.

As the primitive, natural needs are more generalized than the later, higher ones, so are the natural objects, necessary for being, more widely distributed than the later ones. Nature maintains the natural man with his natural needs much more easily than it does the historical, humane man with his civilization, progress and spirit.

The feeling of beauty is the most general feeling of man, and he expands the notion of beauty even to nature and to all its phenomena; accordingly, art, like religion, is more general than science and philosophy.

214

The masses see, in the sensual form of beauty, even the abstract notions of justice and truth, for the notion of beauty comprehends these two.

But the sense of justice, the most historical, noble, and latest, is limited to only a small number of people.

Similarly, there is much more of the primordial stage of unconsciousness than there is of consciousness. The region of consciousness is just as small in comparison to that of unconsciousness as is the bright area of the illuminated to the vast realm of darkness. Only the unconscious is inherited, and, as there is much more of the unconscious in the psyche than there is of the conscious, there is always much more of the inherited than of the acquired; by far the largest part of the psyche of every human being is inherited from the past. This same proportion of consciousness and unconsciousness which exists in the individual soul exists also in human society; there are always very few of those who are aware of social needs and ideals, of the interests and possible paths for the whole society, people and time. So in the history of mankind only a remote and powerful destiny, independent of the human will and consciousness, directs all the great human affairs and effects the general changes of the world. As the highest ideas take shape unconsciously and unwilled in elevated human spirits, so every great idea, every thought of genius, appeared unconsciously and unwilled. No great phenomenon in history resulted from human consciousness and will; the history of mankind is not the product of the conscious will of man; consciousness could never clearly foresee the consequences of any historical event. Every invention, every discovery, had unanticipated results, because it awakened new

215

forces, opened up new avenues and brought about new methods and instruments in the great struggle of historical mankind. All of man's great spiritual and historical acquisitions—religion, language, art, etc.— are not products of his conscious endeavors or desires, but spontaneous and unconscious results of the natural movement and development of things. No great discovery, no great invention in history occurred consciously and intentionally. As Columbus discovered America unintentionally, while looking for something else, and was unable to predict the consequences of his discovery, so were the great laws of science discovered accidentally, unconsciously and without desire.

Since of all things reason is the weakest, since in every society the men of reason constitute the smallest group, since, in fact, only a very small proportion of things can be understood anyway, and since real freedom can be based only upon consciousness and reason, it follows that there is very little of real freedom in the world, but a great deal of blind necessity, a great deal of the "must." The rule of necessity extends over all the regions of the unconscious, and since the unconscious embraces all the inorganic, the organic, and the largest part of human life, the rule of the "must" covers all these fields.

Like consciousness and reason, freedom is only a tiny drop in the ocean of necessity. Dependence is the most general fact of the universe. Since the majority of men act in a given way because they have to, not because they know that this is the way that they ought to act; since, thus, many more actions rest upon the principle of *must* than upon that of *ought* to (necessity rather than freedom), a much smaller proportion of human actions can be classed as moral, humane and free—since real morality is based only upon freedom—than as natural, unwilling and necessitated. Real freedom and morality are as rare among men as are justice and truth. For the large majority of human beings are merely unconscious and unwilling tools of nature, of their society and their time, of their present. The higher the man, the freer is his spirit from external stimuli and impressions from nature, from the present, and from society and circumstances, while the lower the individual, the more intimately is his soul knit to his body, the more he depends on it and serves it, the more he becomes the instrument of the past, of history, and in the same proportion an integral part of the future. As man's spirit comes to depend less and less upon the external world, the further he is from the primordial, natural non-historical life, so the so-called *nihil in intellectu* holds good only for the child and for the primitive man, who receive all their impressions and perceptions from the outside, from nature, from environment and present, and who, accordingly, create all their opinions from these direct impressions and perceptions. The further man is from that primitive life, the more mature he becomes, the deeper he penetrates history, and the higher he is, which is to say, the more he is bound with historical ties, the more of the historical tradition there is in his mind. His knowledge, his notions and ideas become increasingly internal, the results more of history than of his senses. The great historical theories and ideas—gravitation, evolution, law and justice—do not arise from sense impressions or experience but from history. Modern man accepts gravitational theory not as a result of sense perceptions and thought, not because his mind is better developed than that of his predecessors, but

217

because he received the idea of gravitation as a spiritual and historical heritage. Thus, the greater historical progress produces the higher and more mature man, whose spirit is ever freer from the immediate present.

Accordingly, man is free only when he acts independently of the pressure of the present and of his narrow and selfish personal goals. Only such free action is moral, for only real freedom is moral; true morality can be found only in liberty; only a free man can be a moral person. All actions resulting from the "must," from purely natural, selfish and animal motives, have no connection with morality. Since the large majority of people do only what they have to do, since their actions arise from lower, selfish motives, they never rise to freedom, to morality, to the "should." The greater the reasoning power and the area of consciousness, the greater the realm of freedom: Freedom of will is preconditioned by the maturity of reason; freedom develops in history and with history. Freedom grows with progress, with the ever increasing depth of the past, with ever increasing human maturity. Freedom of the will is nothing other than obedience to reason, which erupts with ever greater strength from the increasing depth of time.

Since the earlier is more general and necessary, the earlier a thing, the more general is the need it meets, the more it is needed by an ever growing number of things.

The sun is necessary to the entire solar system, from the planets to man's mind; man is only necessary to himself.

Accordingly, the more something is needed, the more abundant it is, and the more generally distributed. Warmth and air are more necessary than any other factors of life, and they are found everywhere; water is less gen-

218

erally distributed than air, but is more abundant on the whole than other food.

As the earlier is the condition of the later, and is more general than the later, the earlier a thing, the more general a condition of later things it represents. And, since the earlier affects the later, the earlier a thing, the more general and all-embracing is its influence upon all the later.

Since the earlier is more generally distributed—more abundant and more easily obtained than the later—the earlier a thing, the cheaper it is, the later, the more expensive. Objects which satisfy the earliest needs of organic life—air and water—are obtained much more easily and cheaply than items of food. The later, higher goods, which are needed only in later and higher historical societies, are the most expensive. Every acquisition and good of civilization is bought at the price of great misfortunes and struggles; every great truth was obtained only by great sacrifices, only through the efforts of entire centuries.

Likewise, the later, higher religions are much more costly than the earlier, lower ones: Christianity was ransomed only by the blood of its martyrs in the earlier times; later, Protestantism was born through long and harsh struggles of entire peoples. Thus, as civilization progresses, space and time are becoming ever more expensive goods. So also, at the lower levels of history man with his life and acquisitions is cheaper; with the increase of his connections and goods in the historical process, man is becoming ever dearer.

As proportion is the last, highest level of life, proportionality is the briefest moment in the whole process of being.

The deeper one descends from man into nature, the more one finds of the general and common. The earlier a thing, the less proportion it enjoys, the less freedom of movement it has; the later and more developed it is, the more proportion and, with proportion, the more freedom of action it enjoys. Proportion leads to freedom; freedom is the result of proportion. Accordingly, the higher the forms of life, the better the proportion of parts. The more perfect is the proportion of the individual parts, the higher the harmony—the more harmonious is the music of life. Since in the majority of men the sensual, animal and physical prevails over the humane, rational and spiritual, it is no wonder that real freedom, justice, truth and morality cannot be found there. So the highest reason passes, as a slender thread, through an enormous mass of facts and knowledge.

Just as in human thinking justice is rudimentary, occupying a very insignificant place, so it is in modern society; a small minority consumes half of the produce of social labor, just as in ancient times. Thus, there is much more of injustice than of justice: The sum of human misery still far outweighs the total of happiness.

Since there is so little proportion among men, there is little of the good and much evil. Hence in human life the tragic prevails over the comic; everything in man's history—peoples, societies, states, institutions, struggles and revolutions—belongs to the domain of tragedy, while the actors of comedy are few in number; the tragical embraces by far the greater part of man's life and history.

So the inorganic world, with all its forces, stands toward the organic in the same proportion as the organic stands toward man; and as man's physical, sensual, animal existence stands toward the nobility of the spirit, and as those who think stand toward that

one who could understand everything. If this proportion of things were expressed in figures, it would
look, perhaps, somewhat like the following:

$$1,000,000,000,000,000$$
$$1,000,000$$
$$1,000$$
$$10$$
$$1$$

CHAPTER XVIII

Since the earlier is more, and the later less abundant, the earlier a thing is, the more space it occupies; the later, the less.

Just as the uppermost of the earth's strata, upon which all her higher forms of life arose, constitutes a very small part of the earth's mass, so is the part of the earth occupied by organic life very small in comparison to the immensity of her inorganic layers and elements: It is only the surface of the earth, only the thinnest of all the strata of her enormous body.

Of all the organic, man occupies the smallest part, and man's life in general occupies more space than his civilizations; spirit and history are limited to individual points in life and space.

The lowest and earliest stratum of the earth's crust occupies the largest volume, and similarly, touch, the most primitive sense, is the most generally distributed, covering the entire surface of the body, while other, later senses occupy only small parts of it. And in man himself, the bodily, material and animal, occupies much more space than the later humane, than the soul; and the animal soul, in the service of body and life, occupies most of the psyche. And only one organ of the body may be called the organ of the soul and spirit; while the sense organs are numerous and widely distributed.

In the region of the spirit, consciousness is the narrowest and most restricted part; and in the consciousness there is place for only a limited number of presentments at any one time, as the spirit is able to present clearly only a little at any given moment. On the other hand, the region of the unconscious, as earlier, is much larger; the greatest number of thoughts, abstractions and ideas appear unconsciously at first, and only later rise to the light of consciousness.

So the region of beauty is much larger than the area of the spirit. The products of architecture, the first art, occupy much more room than the products of all the other arts together.

Thus, on the map of the human spirit, which is to be elaborated by history, the major mass of the continents will represent religion and poetry; knowledge will appear as smaller countries, while reason will be located only at minute points.

As the earlier occupies more space, the earlier a thing, the larger it is, and the later, the smaller. The magnitude of things is proportional to their priority in time.

As in every animal body the primary (alimentary) organs are larger than all the others, later developed ones, so in every society the food-producing classes are larger than all the other, later, and more highly complex social layers: Production of food and other necessities occupies the greater part of the social energy. And in the same way, the human species is larger than the races, peoples and tribes.

As things appear in the order of their necessity, and the earlier a thing, the more space it needs, it follows that the earlier a thing, the more it is only of space, while the later it is, the more it is in time.

Not only does one study, in all the first sciences,

and in the first phases of all sciences, the spatial relations of things—their motions, etc.—but even in history the first phase is geography, and the greater part of all sciences, for the longest period of their history, is concerned only with things in space. History, the science of the laws of time, occupies the smallest part of the energy of human thought.

Since the earlier is larger and more necessary, the earlier a thing, the more need there is for it in later times; accordingly, the earlier a thing, the larger is the quantity of it that is needed, and the greater the number of later things that will need it.

Since the earlier is more general and occupies more space than does the later, the later things are, the more they are scattered at only a few points in space, and in the progress from matter to spirit, to ever fewer points.

CHAPTER XIX

As the earlier is more general and more common, the earlier a phase of general development, the more common it is, the more things and persons pass through it, while ever smaller numbers of things and people pass through the later phases.

As everything passes through the primordial phase—the inorganic—every man must pass through the phase of the embryo, through the unconscious life of childhood, when he only lives and feels; these first phases of life are common to all human beings, from the lowest to the highest.

So all of mankind passes through the first stage of development, through the age of the natural, savage life; but only its ever smaller individual parts pass through the other, later phases of existence, through the historical process. Just as every man at the beginning of life passes through a period which is without language, so mankind as a whole once passed through that phase, while the historical peoples all entered history with ready, elaborated tongues. In a similar way, tribal life is common to all peoples up to their entrance into history.

Thus do all men pass through the family, and the largest part of mankind with their needs, sympathies and ideas, always stay at the family level. Only individual classes, or a few men rise to the notion of the people, to their interests and needs, while only particular, noble spirits rise to the idea of mankind, to the highest level of humanity and generosity. So only a small number of tribes and peoples develop to real civilization, to the highest level of history, while the great majority of mankind remains always on the lower levels of existence.

So, as previously observed, the history of mankind is a long road, broad at the beginning, and ever narrower toward the end. All mankind passes through the primitive, natural phases of life, but only particular races, tribes, peoples and classes attain the later stages, and only individual spirits pass through the final phases. The further one travels along the road of progress, the narrower the road becomes, the more stragglers drop out, unable to proceed. Only a few powerful and noble spirits progress furthest along the ever narrower and ever more difficult path.

Thus all men pass through the primitive phase of emotion and religion, and the greater part stay at that level, while science and philosophy, being at later and higher points of the spiritual process, are reached by only a few, and the ever fewer, the higher the point of development, the more general and deeper the thought. Religion is the philosophy of the masses, it is the broad highway that all men travel. Science and philosophy are religions of individual spirits, narrow pathways which, the further they go, the less able they are to accommodate large numbers of people.

Thus the circle of reason and consciousness, ideas and theories, is the smallest of all; descending from the height of reason, we begin to enter ever larger circles of feeling, emotion and unconsciousness—of naked existence.

Since the earlier the phases of the process, the more com-

mon they are to all later things; since all things start at the same point, all the later passes along the same way and repeats the development of all that precedes it.

Man, the latest creature, repeats in his development not only the physical, but also the psychic phases of his predecessors. The earlier things being the more common, the primitive psychic forces and characteristics are shared by man with the animals. Even the noblest human spirits pass through the first stages of life, through all psychic phases, rising through life, impulse, emotion, and sensuality, toward the ever purer forms of spirit. And man passes through all the animal phases, the impulses of self-preservation and preservation of the species. Human language as well passes through the phase of interjections and bodily movements in which the animal always remains; man is moved primordially only by physical forces, blind urges and physical needs, on the level at which the animal remains.

Thus every mature man passes through the life phases of earlier man or of the child: In passing through the stage of childhood every man recapitulates all the phases of earlier physical and psychic existence. In the same way the later, higher, historical man passes through the phases of the earlier lower, natural man who remains psychically at the level of the child of the higher man or at the level of the higher man as a child.

Since the higher historical man in the process of his development passes through the phases of the primitive, lower, natural man, the higher historical man passes also all the successive phases through which mankind passed in the long process of its development; he passes again the way of all mankind, so that the way which man has to pass from the first phase of his life to the mature and civilized human being is as long as the road from the first savage epochs to the present heights of mankind, to its present civilization; so that a civilized man passes in his lifetime the entire journey that mankind has made in thousands of years before him, thereby repeating in miniature, and for a brief time, in the development of his own spirit and idea, the entire history of humanity.

Man's intellect, the latest and highest of all his powers, passes through the phases of all the earlier; the history of man's intellect is the history of the world. Since all nature lives only once, it passes through the successive phases of its development only once; and since man is its last creature, since he appeared only after nature had lived all the earlier phases of its life, so that man could not see them nor experience them (as he did not yet exist), and since the later things are, the more they pass through the stages of the earlier, the human intellect lives through all the earlier phases of the life of nature. The successive phases of the human mind correspond to the successive phases of the entire life of nature. And since man's thoughts about things and about the world as a whole developed in the same succession as the things themselves appeared, the ideal, abstract phases, the phases of human reason, correspond to the stages of concrete developments.

And, as in its own history, man's intellect lives through the phases of the life of the entire world, so great individual minds live in their thoughts the life and history of the whole world in advance, not only those phases that the world already passed through but also those through which it is yet to pass: Man's mind shows the way all things will have to travel, the way all earlier things must later pass.

CHAPTER XX

*Since the later phases through which things
and men develop are further and higher, the later
a thing, the longer its course, the further its journey; the earlier a thing, the shorter its way.*

Primordial, lower man passes in life along a much
shorter course than the later, higher, historical man;
the lower the man, the shorter is his life's journey; the
higher the man, the higher and further he must
travel. While the lower man, satisfying the primitive
bodily needs, does not go further, the higher man,
with ever increasing maturity, goes ever further; sens-
ing the higher, later needs, he clambers up to history
and historical living.

So the longest and furthest way is that of the
higher, historical man; the life arcs of the great
human spirits plumb the depths of the world ever
deeper. From naked animal life to the heights of
spirit, to the highest reason and consciousness, is a
much greater distance than between inorganic and
organic. Reason is the highest point the earth can ever
reach through man.

Since all things and human beings pass through the
earliest phases of the process, and since the earlier a
thing, the shorter the way it must travel, it follows that
the shorter the way, the broader, better cleared and
easier it is, since such great numbers of things and
people pass that way. But the further one goes, the

less clear is the pathway and the more difficult to follow. Man's mind and his thought have to pass the longest way of all things and on this latest part of his voyage man has stumbled, fallen and become lost the greatest number of times. As it is difficult for man to overcome the natural inertia of his mind, as it is more difficult for him to strain his reason than his body, so the majority of even those who do use their brains stop with that which is most necessary, and go no further. Hence the majority of even intellectual activities are workmanlike, practical and external.

And the development of the child and of the mass-man is much shorter than that of higher historical man.

Since the earlier phases are experienced by the larger number of things, the earlier is not only shorter in its course, but broader as well; and accordingly, the course of the later is not only longer, but narrower. All men pass through the history of physical life, but fewer and fewer of them pass through all the phases of the development of the spirit.

CHAPTER XXI

As the later depends upon all the earlier, and is
bound to the earlier and the remote, the ties of
later things are ever longer and more remote, and
accordingly, the connections of the earlier are
shorter.

The connections between the plant and the earth
are more intimate than those between earth and man,
while the ties between man's spirit and the earth are
very remote and indirect.

Since the earlier has ever shorter ties, even the movement
of the earlier has ever shorter rhythm. Since the earlier has
ever shorter ties, it follows that the ties of the earlier are ever
stronger, and, accordingly, the ties of the later are ever more
tenuous, and therefore ever more fragile.

The bonds of man's physical life to nature are
much stronger than those of his spiritual life; the ties
of the civilized, historical man are much longer and
finer than those of the primordial man, so that the
movements of the historical man are much freer and
wider. And the threads which are woven through the
history of mankind are far more fragile, far more
subject to snarling and breaking than those which are
woven through the life of nature; this is why so often
in the course of history they become snarled and
broken.

CHAPTER XXII

As the ties of the earlier are shorter, the earlier things are more directly connected; the earlier they are, the closer they are to one another.

The body and life of the animal, and even more of man, are not as direct products of the earth as are plants; they do not stand toward her in such close relationship, they are not so close to the earth, do not receive from her so immediately all they need for maintenance. And the animal soul is more closely bound to the life of the body than is the case with man, and as the animal psyche is always bound to the bodily and sensual, the soul of the animal is much closer to nature and to its processes than is the soul of man. And the lower the man, not only is his psyche more bound to the body and its life in dependence and servitude, but even his spirit is more closely tied to the senses, to direct observations and impressions; the higher the spirit, the freer it is; the less bound to the sensible, external, immediate impressions. So man's first impressions, his first view of the world, are completely bound to the stimuli of external nature; they developed under the direct influence of nature on man's spirit. Similarly, the earlier, the lower the levels of religion, the closer are the deities to man, the more directly they intervene in human destiny, and the more they are bound to the real, the material; as well as at the earlier level of the spirit, knowledge and thought are ever more closely bound to religion. So also the first civilizations are completely bound to external nature, developing directly on the basis of external, natural conditions.

Since the earlier a thing is, the shorter and stronger are its ties; the earlier a thing, the less freedom in movement it has.

CHAPTER XXIII

Since the earlier is ever less complex, ever sim-
pler and with shorter connections, the earlier the
phenomenon, the more uniform it is, the more it is
an indivisible whole.

As the age of myth is the primordial, unitary stage
of the human spirit, so is the human species originally
a unified whole, since all human beings form only one
animal species, although there are several psychic
types.

Accordingly, the later a thing, the more it is only a part,
and the later, the smaller the part.

Since the earlier is ever more one, it has fewer and
fewer parts. And as the earlier is more of one great
Whole, as the earlier is larger, all that is great and
whole can only be seen and understood from an ever
greater distance, that is to say, from an ever increasing height. With the progressive advance of history,
the earlier things withdraw into an increasing distance; they fall into ever greater depths, and they act
from ever greater depths. The first creations can only
be seen from the pinnacles of history. Since the earlier a thing, the larger and more regular it is, all regularity and legality are seen only from the distance,
only from the heights. The greater, the deeper the
regularity, the greater is the distance from which
alone it can be seen; from nearby one can see only
irregularities, only tiny, broken things.

234

As the earlier is ever more only one, the earlier a thing, the smaller the number of times it occurs, lives, appears and disappears. While the human species lives only once (because all the conveniences that enabled it to appear came only once), since it appeared only once and will disappear only once—later forms, tribes and peoples, appear and disappear many times.

Since the earlier exists fewer times than the later, it increases less and less. And since the earlier a thing, the more it is unified, it has fewer causes, conditions and requirements, fewer connections and relations, so that the earlier a thing, the more its life is woven from fewer elements, has fewer and fewer complications and occurrences, changes and attributes. Nature is not mild or severe, merciful or cruel; it contains neither good nor evil; neither justice nor injustice; it is neither truthful nor false, neither beautiful nor ugly; it is neither useful nor harmful, neither medicinal nor poisonous.

Since the earlier has fewer causes and conditions, the earlier a thing, the fewer levels and phases it has in its development, and, accordingly, the less form and the more content. The later a thing, the less content it has, the more form and forms it possesses. And since the root of all later things lies in the preceding ones, it follows that the earlier a thing, the more basic it is, the more it lies at the root of things. The animal sensuality lies at the root of all man's historical features and acquisitions. The root of the development of all soul and spirit is in feeling; as is the striving for truth, justice and reason—the root of religion, law, morality, art, science and philosophy.

CHAPTER XXIV

*Since things settle and place themselves one
upon the other in space in the same succession in
which they appear in time—since the earlier is
always more fundamental—the earlier a thing is,
the deeper is the level to which it settles and
remains.*

As in the stratification of the earth, so also in man,
the primary, natural, animal characteristics, forces
and requirements, lie much deeper than his later, social and historical ones. Thus the instinct of self-
preservation and egoism are much deeper in man's
psyche, and move and direct him from a greater
depth, than do generosity and humaneness, the last
and thinnest strata of the human mind. Since
primordial man with his characteristics and abilities
persists in the masses of historical societies, real civilization and progress rise only on the posterior, higher
strata of society, with the higher men.

*Since the earlier is ever deeper, the earlier is ever more
inward, the later ever more outward; accordingly, the earlier
is more in darkness. And since all the later depends upon all
the earlier, the later a thing, the deeper its roots.* The things
of the world are so situated that the higher one of
them stands, the deeper is the source of its life and
motion. The more advanced is an idea or a theory,
the deeper lie its roots in history. Lesser and lower

thoughts have their roots in the shallow present and they die with their times, while the ideas whose roots are deeper survive the epochs in which they appear, survive their present for ever longer periods.

Since the earlier is more lasting and greater, more independent and necessary, more general and mighty, deeper and more regular, that which is *the earliest,* which pre-exists everything else, *is* in all times, remains after everything else, is only one, occupies all spaces, is always and everywhere, is itself perfect regularity and harmony, is eternal, permanent, unchanging; it is the essence itself; it exists by itself alone, creates everything else, is the cause and condition of itself, is needed by everything later, but does not need anything itself; it is self-sufficient; everything later depends upon it, while it does not depend on anything else; it maintains itself only by itself; from within itself; it creates everything and destroys everything; it is the absolute, it is the perfect truth, the highest reason; it understands everything, nothing can be understood without it.

That *earliest* is and only can be *God.*

PART III

SELECTED
APHORISMS

SELECTED APHORISMS

1

The universe is only a scale of combinations, gradations and proportions of one and the same thing.

2

The whole external world is only an envelope. And when man, after long efforts, succeeds in deciphering the address, he will see that the letter was not mailed to him.

3

Human beings are equal, but only from the height of God, only before God, because from that elevation they are all petty and there is no difference in their pettiness.

4

When the Gods were closer to mankind, tribes and peoples were further from one another; as God became ever more elevated above humanity and ever more distant from it, human beings began to draw ever closer.

5

A dogma is an embalmed thought—dead but whole, live but motionless, soulless but powerful.

6

In the beginning, philosophy is nothing other than a religious heresy.

7

History is the anatomy of time.

8

Unconsciousness does what *must* be, consciousness what *can* be, and conscience what *ought* to be.

9

The deeper the reason, the fewer the keys it needs to open the many doors of the edifice of nature. When it finds a single key, it will discover that it is better not to open the last door at all, but leave it closed.

10

True intelligence, climbing to ever greater heights, looks down into ever greater depths.

11

Great spirits are holidays in the calendar of the history of mankind.

12

Man's thought is the final phase of sunlight, the last and highest form that sunlight assumes, the ultimate vibration of its rays.

13

To come to the conclusion that life is empty one does not have to be a thinker; but to take a deeper look into that emptiness and discover in it something, after all, for that one has to be a philosopher.

14

A talent discerns fine differences among things, a genius fine similarities.

15

A library is a graveyard of minds.

16

Luck is blind, but fate has eyes.

17

They say that everybody forges his own fortune. But destiny gives some people both a hammer and a hot iron, while others must forge it often cold and often with a naked fist.

18

The individual disappears completely: his body disintegrates, his name is forgotten—only his mind remains in the society from which he acquired it and where it developed. Every individual returns the elements of his being to those regions from which he received them: his body to nature, his mind to society.

19

Not man, but mankind is the microcosm, the cosmos in miniature. Only in mankind can all the sides of man's mind and spirit develop. Only mankind is the whole, developing man's body and soul under all conditions and in all circumstances.

20

The masses see only that which can be seen with the eye of the senses. They neither perceive nor wish to perceive the invisible. This is why they can be led only by personalities and not by ideas and why they submit more readily to men than to laws.

21

Of every great idea only the flower and the fruit are visible; the root is always deep in history; the greater the idea, the deeper its root. This is why the crowd, aware only of the perceptible, adores only the success, only the external; it does not see the effort, the labor and the root. Therefore, it attributes the very creation of the idea to him who gave it its final form.

22

A physiognomy is often like a sonorous book title: it promises much but stands for little, and the reverse.

23

Modern society resembles a library in which books are arranged not according to their content and value, but according to their size and binding.

24

In modern society there are three classes of people: 1. those who are silent; 2. those who talk; and 3. those who say something. The first are the most numerous, the last the least.

25

Tragedy belongs to aristocracy, comedy to democracy. As history and civilization descend to the lowlands of life, there is more and more material for the comic. Comedy came into being when the *demos,* the *plebs* raised its head, when the masses appeared in history.

26

The most evident indication that a society is corrupt and decaying is that everything noble in it becomes ridiculous—justice and love, patriotism and humaneness, fidelity and purity, mercy and sincerity.

27

It is harder and more unbearable not to be healthy than to be really sick.

28

The life of primordial men, of children and of the masses reminds one of a clock without hands; one hears the beats of time without knowing what time it is. The same applies to people without recorded history.

29

Tribes and peoples are natural—historical shelters in which immature man becomes the mature man of mankind. They are schools in which the child learns to be an adult.

30

Mature mankind does not need powerful states but free peoples.

31

In order to be a true man, one must not lose oneself either in the father or in the son; either in the husband or in the brother; either in the citizen or in the philosopher; either in the scientist or in the nationalist. One must free oneself from all these ties in order to be a man.

32

True independence, worthy of a free and mature human being, is the independence from people and circumstances and the dependence upon laws alone. That is the objective of all progress and the only possible foundation for a free and humane society.

33

Man is a rebel by nature. His very labor is rebellion, taking away from nature that which she does not give him herself.

34

People stumble only on small stones; they avoid the large ones.

35

In both nature and society people can climb only with their backs bent.

36

Man is a being in whom sometimes even God rejoices but of whom often even the Devil is ashamed.

37

Man is the ultimate form of matter; spirit is the ultimate form of man; it is the matter of history.

38

It is easier to commiserate than to rejoice with others.

39

A proud and noble man never seeks good fortune from destiny or charity from his fellows. He is satisfied when destiny treats him with courtesy and people allow him to go his way in peace.

40

Honest people are a separate race of the human species.

41

People will abandon the paths of wickedness only when they become convinced that virtue is in their interest.

42

Worthier of pity is he who loses his love because of his mind than he who loses his mind because of his love.

43

A friendship that begins in pity usually ends in gossip.

44

Evil is the first tie that links man to man.

45

It is ugly to feel one's happiness in another's unhappiness, but it is uglier to feel one's unhappiness in another's happiness.

46

One of the foundations of a philosophy of life is to make of duty a pleasant habit.

47

It is man's curse to find wisdom when he no longer needs it and bread after he has lost his teeth.

48

If you cannot find the noble and the beautiful in any other way, then observe what is ridiculed by the foolish and jealous. There you will surely find more or less of it.

49

The turning point in one's social upbringing is attained when one is no longer willing or able to be a bore.

50

Fear not only takes away half of a man's strength but gives that half to his enemy.

PART IV

BIBLIOGRAPHY

BIBLIOGRAPHY*

Knežević's Original Books

Principi istorije, Knjiga prva: Red u istoriji, Beograd, Izdanje fonda Dimitrije Nicolića—Belje, Štampano u kraljevskosrpskoj državnoj štampariji, 1898, str. 302.

Principi istorije, Knjiga II: Proporcija u istoriji, Beograd, štampano o trošku Fonda Dimitrije Nikolića—Belje, Štampano u kraljevsko-srpskoj državnoj štampariji, 1901, str. 374.

Dva zakona u istoriji, I. Zakon reda u istoriji, Beograd, Štamparija Svetozara Nikolića, 1904. (Preštampano iz Srpskog književnog glasnika, 1904), str. 77.

Misli, Beograd, 1902, str. 151.

Misli, Beograd, Izdavačka knjižarnica Lazara Markovića, Drugo dopunjeno izdanje, 1914, str. 156.

Misli, Beograd, Izdavačka knjižarnica Gece Kona, Treće dopujeno izdanje, 1925, str. 156.

Misli, U redakciji Pauline Lebl-Albale, S. predgovorom dr Ksenije Atanasijević, Srpska književna zadruga, Kolo XXXIV, (Beograd, 1931), str. 171 (predgovor, str. XXXVI).

Istoriski kalendar, Beograd, 1904, str. 112.

Istoriski dogadjaji, Beograd, drugo izganje, str. 122.

Zakon reda u istoriji, Predgovor V. Vujića. Beograd, Izdavačka knjižarnica Gece Kona, 1920, str. XXIII+171.

Spisi o istoriji—Istorija prema drugim naukama—(Rukopis koji se čuva u Narodnoj biblioteci u Beogradu, R 484).

Misli (Rukopis koji se čuva u Narodnoj biblioteci u Beogradu).

*With a few modifications, this updated Bibliography was adapted from the comprehensive and solid monograph on Knežević by Dr. Kosta Grubačić, cited under "Works about Knežević."

Knežević's Original Articles

Proces istorije čovečanstva i njen odnos prema drugim naukama, članak objavljen u časopisu »Prosvetni glasnik« 1903, br. 2, 3, 4, 5, str. 193–206, 300–314, 424–435, 563–572.

Srazmera u istoriji, jedna glava iz »Principa istorije«, objavljeno u časopisu »Prosvetni glasnik«, 1899, str. 376–381, 444–450.

Zakon reda u istoriji, objavljeno u časopisu »Srpski književni glasnik«, 1904, knjiga XI, str. 190–204, 265–277, 354–366, 438–450, 514–528, 608–616.

Zakon proporcije u istoriji, objavljeno u časopisu »Srpski književni glasnik«, 1904, knjiga XII i XIII, str. 1080–1092, 1151–1162, 1257–1269 i 54–60, 205–213, 347–350, 433–445.

Robert Solisberi, štampano u listu »Odjek« od 23. X. 1902, br. 23.

Luj Blan, štampano u listu »Odjek« od 26. X. 1902, br. 26.

Džems Monroe, štampano u listu »Odjek« od 29. X. 1902, br. 29.

Kamil Kavur, štampano u listu »Odjek«, od 5. XI. 1902, br. 36.

Viljem Gledston, štampano u listu »Odjek« od 9. XI. 1902, br. 40.

Džordž Kaning, štampano u listu »Odjek« od 27. XI. 1902, br. 58.

Knežević's Translations from English, French, German and Russian

O herojima, heroizmu i obožavanju heroja u istoriji, od Toma Karlajla, sa engleskog preveo B. Knežević, Beograd, Srpska književna zadruga 85, štampano u državnoj štampariji kraljevine Srbije, str. I–XV–327.

O socijalizmu, od Šterna, Beograd, Izdanje »Socijalističke biblioteke« Dragiše Lapčevića.

Istorija civilizacije u Engleskoj, od H. T. Bekla. (Preveo Božidar Knežević), Beograd, Izdanje Kolarčeve zadužbine, 1891, str. 375+376+232, ukupno 983, V 8⁰.

O predavanju istorije u srednjoj školi, od N. Karjejeva, (Prevod nije potpisan, ali je ime prevodioca naznačeno u sadržaju) objavljeno u »Prosvetnom glasniku« 1902. godine, str. 566–576 i 674–680 u prvom polgodju, zatim nastavci u sveskama drugoga polgodja, na stranama 32–42, 163–171, 293–302 i 436–449.

Uvod u istoriju Staroga veka, od N. Karjejeva. (Ime prevodioca naznačeno je u »Sadržaju«). Objavljeno u »Prosvetnom glasniku«, 1903. godine, str. 499–516 i 603–628.

BIBLIOGRAPHY

Evolucija rada u staroj Grčkoj, od Pola Giroa, (Ime prevodioca naznačeno u »Sadržaju«), objavljeno u »Prosvetnom glasniku«, 1904. godine, prvo polgodje, str. 149–170.
Ogledi, od T. B. Makoleja, Preveli B. Knežević i V. Savić, Beograd, Srpska književna zadruga, kolo XXI, br. 143, str. 187.

Works About Knežević
(mostly articles)

Anonim, Knežević Božidar (neki kratki bibliogr. podaci o Boži Kneževiću). Bibliografija rasprava, članaka i književnih radova, I. Zagreb, Izdanje i naklada Leksikografskog zavoda FNRJ, 1956.
Anonim, Božidar Knežević, Pravda, Beograd 2/1905, 44, 3.
Anonim, Božidar Knežević, Samouprava, Beograd, 1905, 42, 3.
Anonim, Principi istorije B. Kneževića, Nada, knj. IV. 1898, str. 192.
Anonim, Principi istorije od Bože Kneževića, Delo, knj. XVIII, 1898, str. 349.
Anonim, Misli Bože Kneževića, Delo, knj. XXIII, 1902, str. 449.
Anonim, Misli Bože Kneževića, Delo, knj. XXIV, 1902, str. 308.
Anonim, Boža Knežević, Istoriski kalendar, Delo, knj. XXXIII, 1904, str. 142–143.
Anonim, Zakon reda u istoriji, od Bože Kneževića, Delo, knj. XXXI, 1904, str. 286–287.
Anonim, Boža Knežević, Bosanska vila, 1905, knj. XX, str. 80.
Anonim, Boža Knežević, Brankovo kolo, 1905, knj. XI, str. 256.
Anonim, Boža Knežević, Delo, 1905, knj. 34, str. 431–432.
Anonim, Boža Knežević, Književna nedelja, 1905, knj. II, br. 20, str. 96.
Anonim, Dvadesetpet godina smrti Bože Kneževića, »Politika« od 6. marta 1930.
Anonim, Misli Bože Kneževića, Zivot i rad, 1931, knj. IX, str. 1270–1271.
Anonim, Aforizam Bože Kneževića »Politika« od. 13. III. 1960.
Atanasijević, dr Ksenija: Božidar Knéživić, in »Penseurs yougoslaves«, Belgrade, Bureau central de Presse, 1937, p. 136–184.
Atanasijević dr Ksenija, O Božidaru Kneževiću, Vreme, 6–8 januara 1924.
Atanasijević dr Ksenija, Ličnost Božidara Kneževića, Zivot i rad, 1930., knj. V., str. 241–245.

BIBLIOGRAPHY

Atanasijević dr Ksenija, Metafizika i etika Božidara Kneževića, Volja, april 1930, knj. I., sv. 1, str. 15–18.

Atanasijević dr Ksenija, Božidar Knežević, Predgovor »Mislima«, Beograd 1931, str. XXXVI.

Atanasijević dr Ksenija, Bibliografija radova Božidara Kneževića, Život i rad, 1932, knj. XII, str. 1119–1120.

Atanasijević dr Ksenija, Skerlić o Božidaru Kneževiću, Život i rad, 1934. knj. XIX. str. 646–649.

Atanasijević dr Ksenija, Nekoliko pojedinosti o životu i umiranju Božidara Kneževića, Povodom tridesetpetogodišnjice smrti plemenitog mislioca. Pravda, br. 12657, 28. januara 1940.

Atanasijević dr Ksenija. Pedesetogodišnjica smrti filozofa Božidara Kneževića. Republika (Beograd), br. 487. od 1. III. 1955.

Banović Aleksandar. Religiozna filozofija Bože Kneževića, Hrišćansko delo, Skoplie. 1939. Godina V. sveska 3.

Banović Aleksandar, Boža Knežević i Karlajl, Danica, 1940, str. 10–12.

Blagojević Desimir, Dvadesetpet godina od smrti velikog našeg mislioca Božidara Kneževića. Pravda. 4. marta 1930.

Bogdanović Milica. Božidar Knežević filozof istorije, Misao, knj. XLII, 1933, str. 345–382.

Carnegie Andrew: Carstvo poslova. Beograd. »Dositije Obradović« štamparija Ace M. Stanojevića, 1904, str. VIII-+189++(2.). (Moto dela: »Pošten rad—molitva bogu« (iz »Misli« B. Kneževića)).

D. M. Dvadesetpetogodišnjica smrti Božidara Kneževića, Pregled, 1930, knj. V, str. 317.

Dragutinović M. K., Boža Knežević (1862–1905), Nastavnik, 1905, knj. XVI, str. 157–158.

Gavrilović, Žarko: Božidar Knežević, Čovek i istorija, Redakcija i predgovor Dragana Jeremića, izdanje Matice srspske i SKZ, Novi Sad—Beograd, 1972, str. 331.; Teološki pogledi, 4' 72.

Gligorić Velibor, Neohumanisti, Stožer; br. 9–10, str. 243–250, septembar–oktobar 1931. God. II, Beograd.

Grubačić, Kosta: Božidar Knežević. Monografija o znamenitom srpskom filozofu istorije. Sarajevo, »Veselin Masleša«, 1962, str. 205.

Jeremić, M. Dragan: Boža Knežević. Povodom pedesetogodišnjice smrti. Savremenik, Beograd, god. I, maj 1955., str. 598–604.

Jeremić, M. Dragan: Filosof i književnik Božidar Knežević. Danas, Beograd, god. II, br. 21, 28. februar 1962.

254

BIBLIOGRAPHY

J . . ., Boža Knežević, Principi istorije, Prosvetni glasnik, 1898, knj. XIX, str. 596–599.

Jovanović Živorad P., Dodatak bibliografiji (dr. Jovan Skerlić, Istorija nove srpske književnosti), Beograd 1953, str. 510.

Jovanović Zivorad P., Božidar Knežević, Letopis Matice srpske, Godina 131, Decembar 1955, knj. 376, sv. 6, str. 657–660.

Knežević Milivoje, Dvadesetpetogodišnjica smrti Bože Kneževića, Književni sever, 1930, knj. VI, str. 107–109.

Knežević Milka, Život mojih roditelja (rukopis u Narodnoj biblioteci u Beogradu, R 485⁰)

Kostić Dragutin, »Vreme« od 28. III. 1929., pod naslovom: »Šta više vredi u životu: malo duha ili mnogo filozofije?

Kovačević Božidar, O Boži Kneževiću, Život i rad, 1928., knj. II., str. 614–616.

Lazarević Luka, Boža Knežević, Pravda, 16. septembra 1933, br. 10368.

L(ukić) A., Život Božidara Kneževića protekao je tiho i bez prijatelja. Supruga B. Kneževića priča nam o uspomeni na ovog našeg zaslužnog čoveka, Pravda, 3. XI. 1935.

M. M. Na zaboravljenom grobu Božidara Kneževića o tridesetpetogodišnjici njegove smrti—parcela br. 47, grob br. 373, Vreme, 28 mart 1940.

M. M. M., Bog u misli Bože Kneževića, Srpski narod, br. 8, 24. jula 1942.

Mala enciklopedija Prosvete. Beograd. 1959.

Matić Svetozar: Boža Knežević, Misli. »Novi život« 1925, knj. XXIV, br. 12, str. 383.

Milošević Miloš, Božidar Knežević i obnova duha, Vreme, 27–30. aprila 1940.

Minerva, Leksikon, Zagreb, 1936.

M. V. Zakon reda u istoriji od Bože Kneževića, Srpski književni glasnik, 1921. knj. III, str. 239–240.

Nedeljković, Dušan: Filosof Božidar Knežević. Letopis Matice srpske, Novi Sad, god. 138, knj. 390, sv. 4, oktobar 1962, str. 255–271.

Nedeljković dr Dušan, Naša filozofija u borbi za socijalizam, Beograd, Izdanje Naučne knjige, 1952 (na str. 16).

Nikolajević Dušan S.: Boža Knežević, Pravda, 1 marta 1905, br. 52.

Nikolajević Dušan S.: Boža Knežević, Brankovo kolo, 1907, knj. XIII, str. 541–551, 597–600, 633–635, 660–662.

BIBLIOGRAPHY

Nikolajević Dušan S.: Božidar Knežević ka novim duhovnim vidicima, Beogradske opštinske novine, 1936, 54, str. 108–110.

Nikolajević Dušan S.: Misao Klemansoa i Bože Kneževića, Beogradske opštinske novine, 1936, 54 str. 646–648.

Novaković S. Uspomene na poslednje dane života Bože Kneževića »Srpski narod«, br. 8, od 27. februara 1943.

Ostojić K., O egzistencijalizmu u filozofiji Božidara Kneževića, Nedeljne informativne novine, br. 193, od 12. septembra 1954.

P(avlović) M(ilorad): Ocena Bože Kneževića, Republika, 13. oktobra 1953.

P(avlović) M(ilorad): Boža Knežević i čačanski trgovac, Republika, 11. oktobra 1955.

Pavlović Milorad (Mile): Beleške iz starih beležnica (rukopis u Narodnoj biblioteci u Beogradu, R 465).

Pešić Srećko J., Istina Božidara Kneževića, Skoplje, Stamparija »Južna Srbija«, 1935, str. 80.

Petrović Milorad M., Anegdote iz života srpskih književnika. Boža Knežević. Beogradske novine. 21. oktobra 1917 (?).

Petronijević Branislav: Principi istorije, knjiga prva. Red u istoriji. Napisao Boža Knežević. Delo, 1898, knj. XIX. str. 491–506.

Petronijević Branislav: Božidar Knežević, Politika, februara 1905.

Petronijević Branislav: Članci i studije (Boža Knežević), Beograd, 1920, knjiga II.

Petronijević Branislav: Članci i studije, Beograd, 1922, knjiga III.

Popović Vladan D.: O egzistencijalizmu u filozofiji Bože Kneževića, Glasnik, službeni list Srpske pravoslavne crkve, maj 1954.

Popović D.: Boža Knežević kao direktor čačanske gimnazije, Politika 14. oktobra 1937. (Ukoliko je to Popović S. Dragomir on je autor i teksta o istoj temi, a koji je objavljen u »Spomenici čačanske realne gimnazije 1837–1937«).

Popović Zarija R.: Iz života Bože Kneževića. Kćerino krštenje. Venac, 1932, knj. XVIII, str. 133–135.

Popović Zarija R.: Boža Knežević u anegdotama, Venac, 1933, knj. XVIII, str. 358–362.

Popović Mihajlo (o Boži Kneževiću), Enciklopedija Jugoslavije, sv. 3, str. 334.

Popović dr Nikola, Naš dug Božidaru Kneževiću velikom srpskom misliocu, Srpski narod, 14. novembra 1942.

BIBLIOGRAPHY

Popović dr Nikola, Boža Knežević i Djovani Batista Viko, Srpski narod, 9. januara 1943.

(Radojičić Djordje S..): Da li se sačuvao lik srpskog filozofa Božidara Kneževića? Politika od 29. i 30. oktobra 1955.

Radojičić N., Srpska istoriografija (St. Stanojević, Narodna enciklopedija, II, str. 69.

Ristić, Radomir: Prilozi za biografiju Božidara Kneževića, Prilozi za književnost, jezik, istoriju i folklor, Beograd, knj. XXVIII, sv. 1–2, 1962. str. 80–92.

Savković Miloš, Boža Knežević i moderna umetnost, Misao 1930, knj. XXXIV, str. 1–8.

Savković Miloš, Lična drama Bože Kneževića, Misao, 1930, knj. XXXIII, str. 319–328.

Skerlić dr Jovan, Misli od Bože Kneževića, Srpski književni glasnik, knj. VI, 1902, str. 116–127.

Skerlić dr Jovan: Boža Knežević, Srpski književni glasnik, 1905, knj. XIV, str. 398–400.

Skerlić dr Jovan: Pisci i knjige I, Beograd, 1922.

Skerlić dr Jovan, Božidar Knežević, Istorija nove srpske književnosti, Beograd 1953.

Spomenica čačanske realne gimnazije 1837–1937, Čačak 1938, (neki podaci o Boži Kneževiću koje je, verovatno, napisao Dragomir S. Popović).

Stajić Vasa: Misli Bože Kneževića, Kolo 1902, knj. IV, str. 218–222.

(Stevanović Pavle): Božidar Knežević, Zakon reda u istoriji, Novi život, 1921, knj. V, br. 7, str. 222–223.

Stojanović dr Dušan: Božidar Knežević i engleska misao, Srpski književni glasnik, 1940, knj. LX, str. 43–48.

Sveznanje, Leksikon, Narodno delo, Beograd, 1937.

Tasić Djordje: Boža Knežević sa gledišta sociologije, Politika, 23–26. aprila 1938.

Tomashevich George Vid: Božidar Knežević-a Yugoslav Philosopher of History (objavljeno u časopisu »The Slavonic and East European Review«, vol. XXXV, N⁰ 85, ed. University of London, June 1957, S. 443–461).

Trivunac Miloš: Boža Knežević čovek i mislilac, Godišnjak Srpske kraljevske akademije, 1939, str. 153.

Vujić Vladimir: Božidar Knežević, Predgovor knjizi »Zakon reda u istoriji«, Beograd, 1920, str. XXIII.

BIBLIOGRAPHY

Vujić Vladimir: »Misli« Božidara Kneževića, Srpski književni glasnik, 1925, knj. XVI, str. 395–396.

Vujić Vladimir: O Božidaru Kneževiću (1862–1905), Srpski književni glasnik, 1925, knj. XVI, str. 417424.

Vujić Vladimir: Lik Božidara Kneževića, Narodna odbrana 1930, knj. V, str. 325.

Vujić Vladimir: Misli Božidara Kneževića, Narodna odbrana, 1932, knj. VII, str. 140–141.

Vulić Nikola, Istorija kao nauka, Glas Srpske kraljevske akademije, 1922, str. 49–66.

Zega Nikola, Uspomena na Božu Kneževića, Život i rad, 1934, knj. XIX, str. 921–925.

Zorić, Pavle: Božidar Knežević, u knjizi »Članci«, Cetinje, »Narodna knjiga«, str. 103–117, 1956.

Z(orovavelj), Kneževićev krug, Srpski narod, br. 8, 27, februara 1943.

Živančević Mih. M., Božidar Knežević, Povodom 25 godišnjice od njegove smrti, Pravda, 5. marta 1930.